The Japanese Linguistic Landscape

JAPAN LIBRARY

The Japanese Linguistic Landscape
Reflections on Quintessential Words

Nakanishi Susumu

TRANSLATED BY
Ryan Shaldjian Morrison

Japan Publishing Industry Foundation for Culture

Note to the reader:
In this book, long vowels in Japanese are indicated by the use of macrons, except in commonly known place names and words already adopted into English. All Japanese names appearing in this book are given in Japanese order with family name first.

The Japanese Linguistic Landscape: Reflections on Quintessential Words
By Nakanishi Susumu. Translated by Ryan Shaldjian Morrison.
Photographs by Nakanishi Kimiko.

Published by
Japan Publishing Industry Foundation for Culture (JPIC)
3-12-3 Kanda-Jinbocho, Chiyoda-ku, Tokyo 101-0051, Japan

First English edition: August 2019

This book is a translation of *Utsukushii Nihongo no Fūkei* (TANKOSHA PUBLISHING, 2008, 2013) and selections of Part I and II in *Kotoba no Kokoro* (TOKYO SHOSEKI CO., LTD., 2016).
Selections from *Kotoba no Kokoro* Part I first appeared in the following publications.
  Haruka Purasu (Gyosei, April 2007 to October 2011)
Selections from Part II originally appeared in the following writings.
  "Kotogotoku Karuki Hai Nari" in *Kyōiku Tenbō* (Japan Educational Research Institute, November 1989)
  "Hana Nehan" (*Chūnichi Shimbun*, March 29, 2005)
  "Shinran no Kotoba" in *Shinran to wa Nani ka* (Kodansha, April 2011)
  "Toku o Tsume" (*Kōmei Shimbun*, January 29, 2012)
  "Hitotsu o Eru Koto wa Hitotsu o Ushinau Koto demo Aru" (*Kōmei Shimbun*, July 15, 2012)

English publishing rights arranged directly with the author Nakanishi Susumu.

Printed in Japan
ISBN 978-4-86658-068-5
https://japanlibrary.jpic.or.jp/

CONTENTS

CHAPTER TWO
Words about the Four Seasons and Living Things 105

CHAPTER THREE
Words about the Human Heart 193

CHAPTER FOUR
Essays on Modes of Living 279

Foreword

I find it most amusing that when you read through *Tsurezuregusa* (*Essays in Idleness*, 1330–1332)—the famous collection of essays written in the Kamakura period (1185–1333) by the priest Yoshida Kenkō (1284–1350)—you come upon a passage in Episode 22 where the priest laments that the contemporary language keeps growing more and more debased, that people no longer know how to write letters, that ordinary spoken language has steadily coarsened, and so forth.

In a similar passage in Episode 262 of her famous book of essays *Makura no Sōshi* (*The Pillow Book*, ca. 1002)—written in the middle of the Heian period (794–1192), an era that Yoshida Kenkō nostalgically refers to as the "old days" (*mukashi*)—Sei Shōnagon (ca. 966–ca. 1025) indignantly laments the fact that people nowadays have a bad habit of using words that omit the syllable *to*, such as *senzuru* instead of *sen to suru* (to intend to do) or *iwanzuru* instead of *iwan to su* (to intend to do).

What are we to make of these similar complaints? Should we simply assume that the only truly beautiful and correct language was that used by the first humans, Adam and Eve?

Of course, nobody knows what sort of language Adam and Eve spoke.

The name I have given to this tendency toward nostalgia for past language and contempt for the current vernacular is *gengo massekan*, or the "view that language has reached a degenerate age." This eschatological argument is a linguistic version of the idea that we have entered the *mappō*—the degenerate latter days of Buddhist law—and must wait for the bodhisattva Maitreya to come save us, as prophesied by the historical Buddha.

However, no matter how hard governments try to regulate its usage, and whether or not Maitreya appears, language will do as it pleases. Unlike the dog who obediently takes orders from his master, language is a cat. If language could speak, it would no doubt declare, "I am a cat!" (*Wagahai wa neko de aru*), like the feline narrator of Natsume Sōseki's great Meiji-era novel.

Our relationship with language is analogous to our relationship with cats. No matter how hard we try to tame or control language, it inexorably changes over time. Bemoaning that inescapable reality is pointless.

A certain friend of mine—an amusing French fellow—has a habit of using the anachronistic expression *sayō de gozarimasuru* instead of the modern equivalent *sō desu* (that is so) whenever he talks with Japanese people. I imagine this is because he learned Japanese by studying Edo-period literature. Everyone who meets him finds his peculiar charm most endearing.

This doesn't mean, of course, that I am willing to stand by and watch language devolve into ever weirder permutations. The *ra-nuki* words that eliminate the necessary *ra* syllable—where one says *tabereru* (to be able to eat) rather than *taberareru*—strike me as insufferable, for instance. And I also wish that people would pronounce the word 憧憬 (longing, aspiration) as *shōkei* rather than *dōkei*, which has been more common since the Meiji period. But when you try to make a last-stand defense across the entire landscape of language, there are times when you simply can't hold the line. For example, the original and correct reading of 滑稽 (humorous, absurd, comical)—customarily pronounced *kokkei*—is *kakkei*, which was heard for centuries. But if you were to pronounce it as *kakkei* today, you'd indeed sound most *kokkei*.

So how should we comport ourselves vis-à-vis language, then? I suppose all we can do is avoid vulgar trends while still acknowledging that languages are fated to change. Rather than clinging doggedly to the ways of the past, we should insist on using language that lies one step behind the times. Following this advice, I think, will make you a splendid practitioner of beautiful language.

In fact, this thing we call *ningen no hin*—"human refinement" or "grace of character"—can be achieved only if we are are precisely one step behind the times.

Kakkei is too far behind the times for anyone to advocate its return. *Shōkei*, however, is just one step behind. To me, that gives it a kind of elegance.

Come to think of it, this notion of trailing exactly "one step behind" applies to all languages, not just Japanese. British English, for instance, possesses more grace than modern American English—yet standard American English has more grace than American vernacular slang. And so it continues, right on down the line.

At any rate, these are the circumstances that came to mind when I received a request from a great friend, Hattori Tomohiko of Tankosha Publishing, to address the subject of beauty in the Japanese language (*utsukushii Nihongo*) and describe the contours of its linguistic landscape (*fūkei*).

I should add that a beautiful Japanese word is beautiful regardless of when it first appeared in Japan's history. With that in mind, I mix words of all ages into my discussion.

Modern Japanese is made up of two modes: old and new. My aim in this book is to show how the essence of the Japanese language runs consistently through both. My hope is that readers will come to understand that the issue of beauty in language does not depend on whether a word or expression is old or new.

Recently, I happened to see a well-known foreign TV personality on a Japanese program. With a glum face, he said: "Everyone's always talking about how Japanese has so many beautiful words, so many lovely words—but that's nonsense. It just has *old* words, *antiquated* words!"

Such misunderstandings are common among foreigners who learn Japanese. But learning to discern beauty and ugliness in a language requires more than memorizing vocabulary and grammar. It means cultivating perception and accumulating experience. Only by immersing yourself in a language—not simply studying it as a means of communication—can you begin to appreciate that language's true beauty.

I hope this book will attract a broad range of readers, and that those readers will find it interesting and enjoyable, regardless of whether their mother tongue is Japanese.

When I was a boy, I had the following memorable experience.

As I discuss in this book, Japanese-English dictionaries often translate the Japanese word *koharu-biyori* as "Indian summer." On page 126, I describe how this brought a sigh to my lips: "*What on earth is that supposed to mean?* I'd wondered with a sigh." Another dictionary provided a helpful explanation of the word as "a period of warm or mild dry weather in the northern United States in late autumn or early winter."

My sigh came from my astonishment to discover that language could hew so closely to the workings of nature. Both words—*koharu-biyori* and "Indian summer"—express distinct natural phenomena that occur in their respective regional climes. But what they share is that each expresses this crazy anomaly of a warm day in winter.

The issue, then, is how these two words manage to convey the same insanely irregular character of these natural phenomena. Surely there must be something for us to take in from these two terms that employ different means to express similar phenomena.

There is another experience from my youth that I recall vividly. Flipping through my dictionary, I stumbled upon the English word *highwayman*, which was translated into Japanese as *oihagi*, meaning "highway robber." The word seemed to my young mind a kind of riddle: after all, there were no real highways in Japan at that time, let alone the kind of motorized society that we inhabit today. At the time, my only access to most words in the dictionary was through my imagination; this made the word *highwayman* all the more intriguing. In no time, I started tossing the word *highwayman* around at every opportunity.

My dictionary now happens to provide a useful explanation for *highwayman*: "Long ago, the highway robbers (*oihagi*) used to haunt the main roads on horseback." But at the time, the thought that the "main roads" (*kōdō*) of old could correspond to a modern "highway" did not occur to me.

I suppose that all words reside in our imaginations, in a sense: they occupy a kind of dream space.

And when you figure in our capacity for *kandō*—to respond deeply, with immediacy, to language and the radiance therein—what could be more wonderful? As I mention on page 62 of this book (*kazahana*), the experience of being deeply moved is something like "the distinct sensation of having a word radiate before me in a kind of sublime light."

Even for those who take up Japanese as a foreign language, then, there is nothing odd or mysterious about the notion that they, too, will experience that same exact emotional response.

An American friend of mine—an adept Japanese speaker who is also highly versed in classical Japanese literature—once said something that stuck with me. After finally figuring out how to translate the exclamatory particle *kamo* that abounds in classical poetry (especially at the end of a poem), he told me that he felt a perceptible twinge of anxiety in the word *kamo*, tilting his head with a smile.

Listening to him, I found myself nodding in agreement. The first thing that came to mind was that verbal mannerism of today's youth, who often break their thoughts off midsentence with a *kamo ne*—a shortened version of *sō kamo shirenai* (it may be so). The *kamo* of *kamo ne* is often said to be completely different from the *kamo* of classical literature, which connotes an exclamation of emotion. The more pedantic teachers of Japanese language will surely take issue with my "conflation" of the two *kamo*. But in reality, it is highly probable that the interrogative participle *ka* in fact gave birth to the exclamatory *kamo*—and, by extension, the *kamo ne* we hear today.

If my astute American friend had simply grown up speaking Japanese, his realization probably would have never come to light. Acquiring a command of the language through study was the only way he could have discovered foundations of the lexicon's fundamental stages, which native speakers are often oblivious to.

When you think about how non-native speakers can be more attuned to a language's intricacies than native speakers often are, you can see how our habit of distinguishing languages along regional and national borders is no longer meaningful. Naturally, the larger gestalt—geographical climate, everyday customs, and other region-specific qualities—has a tremendous effect on the formation of language. Even as we acknowledge this larger framework of the elements populating everyday life, however, the entire world should share in the universal essence of words, which have a profound influence on our most vital ways of living.

To my mind, a translator is someone who masterfully perceives those intricacies and adroitly navigates between two poles: the particular and the universal. It is through the work of a skillful translator that languages can transcend their borders and become the shared domain of humanity as a whole—and ultimately lay the foundation for lasting world peace.

chapter ONE

Words about Nature

Earth, Sky, Wind, Water, and Fire

Komoriku

■ Secluded Mountainous Regions

W ritten with the Chinese characters 隠 (hiding) + 国 (country), a *komoriku* refers to a topographical region surrounded by mountains, secluded from the outside world.

Since antiquity, the Hatsuse mountains in the old province of Yamato (present-day Nara Prefecture) were called the *komorikuni no hatsuse*, epitomizing these secluded, mountain-nestled *komoriku*.

Japan is a mostly mountainous country; nearly seventy percent of the total land area is uninhabitable due to that topography. It is only natural that there are so many small *komoriku* spaces between mountains. When you peer into the spaces between mountains, you're sure to find *komoriku* in abundance.

What largely determines whether a spot qualifies as a *komoriku* is the scale of the area, interestingly. Even the vast old Yamato province, from a certain perspective, looks just as the *Kojiki*[1] famously describes it: "the mountains are green partitions lying layer upon layer nestled among the mountains—how beautiful is Yamato!" (*tatanazuku / aogaki / yamagomoreru / Yamato shi uruwashi*). Yamato, though expansive, is an example of a secluded *komoriku*, enclosed by mountains—and that *komoriku* identity is what made its defenses so tight and secure. Knowing this, the imperial sovereigns of old wisely chose the region as their base.

And yet, there is another condition that defines a *komoriku*. The area must—at the very least—have enough water for its inhabitants to survive. In the lands with long histories as small hamlet settlements, there were routinely

---

1. *Kojiki* (Records of Ancient Matters, the oldest extant chronicle in Japan, dating from 711–712)

mountains offering water sources, called *mikumari-yama*; a certain fixed, steady amount of water output was likely present.

One example is old Yoshino province, a small, autonomous region that runs along the banks of Yoshino River, one mountain range removed from the ancient village of Asuka. You would never expect, looking from the Asuka side, that there would be an independent settlement over the mountain—but Yoshino had what it needed for subsistence. In addition to its secluded location, it fit the *komoriku* requirement of a water source from the mountains—and a water deity is even enshrined there.

In short, *komoriku* refers to a small, separate space that met the survival needs of its residents, protected them from outside threats, and revealed a distinct natural beauty.

To put it in the terms that Carl Hermann Busse used in his poem "Über den Bergen,"[2] *komoriku* points to some unknown utopia that lies under the "sky over and beyond the mountains yonder" (*yama no anata no sora*).

Finally, I should note that there is another term with similarities to *komoriku*: *kakuresato*. This term, which literally translates to "hidden village," possesses none of the enclosed autonomy implied by *komoriku*. Rather, it simply refers to any place that is invisible to the human eye. As such, it lacks the sense of satisfaction and fulfillment that *komoriku* connotes.

---

2. "Über den Bergen," included in the great symbolist poetry anthology *Kaichōon* (Sound of the Tide, 1905) as "Yama no anata"

Komoriku

こもりく

Tatanazuku

■ Folded Layers of Mountains

*T*atanazuku refers to the way the mountain ranges appear to pile atop one another, one after the other, from a distance. *Tata* is the same *tata* that is found in the word *tatami*, the traditional floor mats in Japanese-style rooms.

I suppose the most famous instance of *tatanazuku* is the one in the *tanka* poem I cited in the previous entry, written by that celebrated hero of antiquity—Yamato Takeru no Mikoto[3]—as he gazed upon the Yamato region (present-day Nara Prefecture):

Yamato wa	Yamato is
kuni no mahoroba	the highest part of the land,
tatanazuku	the mountains are green partitions
aogaki	lying layer upon layer,
yamagomoreru	nestled among the mountains—
Yamato shi uruwashi	how beautiful is Yamato![4]

(Kojiki)

In this poem, Yamato Takeru evocatively depicts the way mountains form stacks of earth in close range, as though a green hedge had encircled the whole of the Yamato area.

In the prehistoric Jōmon period,[5] Japanese people would search the mountains for game and other sustenance. They revered the close-knit stacks of mountains, too, for their superlative ability to serve as a protective wall against outside invaders.

The region of old Yamato, ensconced by such mountains, is home to an abundance of thunder and striking skies, the clouds overhanging the mountains

---

3. Yamato Takeru no Mikoto (ca. 72–114) 4. See note 1 on page 301
5. Jōmon period (ca. 10,000–400 [or 300] BCE)

creating an endless series of beautiful, kaleidoscopic changes.

Those vistas are only possible thanks to *tatanazuku* mountains.

There is also a *waka* poem in Book 3 of the *Man'yōshū*[6] by the great poet Kakinomoto no Hitomaro.[7] In the poem, he describes the flesh of a woman as *tatanazuku nigihada*, which might be translated into English as "soft, supple skin." This might seem shocking if you simply take *tatanazuku* to signify the look of a mountain range. But there was also, in fact, the popular belief that saw the mountain as a sacred goddess. Setting aside the intricacies of that description for the time being, one can see how the aesthetic sensibilities of the premodern Japanese—who saw man and nature in a way that transcended their respective differences—are remarkable in and of themselves, above all.

The woman whose flesh Hitomaro praised in his poem no doubt exhibited both an abundance of beautiful voluptuousness and an expansive, magnanimous sense of reassurance. The radiant glow of her smooth skin, her supple curves—all those physical-formal attributes come together in verse to span the divides between nature and man in a deeply affecting way.

Guy de Maupassant's oeuvre includes a famous short story called "Boule de Suif,"[8] which was translated into Japanese as *Shibō no katamari*. This rather uninspired translation simply means "clump of fat." The story's female protagonist is a young prostitute whom the men around her see as a mere object, a "clump of fat," as they called her. Compared to that inelegant term, *tatanazuku* brims with affection and adulation for the female body.

When we consider the sheer variety of expressions of female beauty in Japanese, including *tatanazuku*, we cannot but admire the language's singular ability to transpose the things of this world (*mono*) into the keys of the mind and heart (*kokoro*).

---

6. *Man'yōshū* (*The Ten Thousand Leaves*, the last poem written in 759, Japan's oldest poetry anthology)
7. Kakinomoto no Hitomaro (active late seventh century)   8. "Boule de Suif" (1880)

Ubusuna

The Land of One's Birth

enoting the land of one's birth, *ubusuna* is usually written with the Chinese characters for *birth* 産 and *soil* 土. These days, however, we usually encounter the term in the context of *ubusuna-gami*, local guardian spirits. The traditional custom of taking a newborn baby to meet the guardian spirits at the local Shinto shrine still exists today.

Just why we call one's place of birth by this name, *ubusuna* (literally, baby + sand), remains in the realm of conjecture. Yet we do know that the first part of the term—*ubu*—is related to the act of being born, as evidenced in common terms such as *ubugi* (baby clothes), *ubuyu* (a newborn's first bath), and *ubugoe* (a newborn's first cry). Relatedly, we also know that the verb for bringing something into being is *umu*. Hence, *ubu* and *umu* are clearly interrelated terms, pairs of a single unit.

The second part of the term—*suna*—seems to be related to the notion of sacred land. The *na* of *suna* has long been associated with earth or soil (*tochi*). And since *su* was often used as a variation of *sa*, we can surmise that *suna* probably means something akin to *seichi*, or "holy land."

What is certain, however, is that the term *ubusuna* originated in the sixth century CE—and fourteen centuries is a long time for a word to survive. That longevity no doubt owes a great deal to the notion of birthplace, one that Japanese people have long imbued with great importance.

The issue of where one is born has always been a central concern for the Japanese. Even today, people ask each other, *O-kuni wa* (What is your *o-kuni*)?

うぶすな

Kuni is generally translated as "country," but in this case, the term refers to one's home region. The fact that the subject of one's birthplace still comes up in conversation testifies to the enduring power of this legacy.

Each of us is born from this great earth, this *daichi*, and it is to this great earth that each of us shall return someday. I strongly believe that we each conceive our own self-identity according to the land of our birth, which, in my view, constitutes a fundamental basis for all human life.

The word *ubusuna* thus takes on a certain weight, a certain richness—a sanctity that is hard to deny.

I noted above that people today encounter the term *ubusuna* mostly in the sense of *ubusuna-gami*, or the guardian spirits of one's hometown. In that sense, *ubusuna* also serves the role of connecting us to the spirit world.

We are a nation of people who have long resided in small, fragile abodes built of paper and wood—"rabbit huts" (*usagi goya*), as they are often called. That sense of impermanence has given us an uncanny lightness, a nimbleness that allows us to pack up and move quickly from one residence to the next—and our spry mobility has contributed greatly in the making of modern Japan, too.

Still, I hope that, even in the midst of our modern, uprooted mode of life, each of us will find a way to preserve this sense of *ubusuna*, to uphold the sanctity of one's place of birth, to feel its importance deep in our bones. If we lose that connection to our native soil, our lives will be no more durable than castles in the sand.

Kagiroi

■ Hot Waves Shimmering in Air

agiroi is a noun that describes the soft, shimmering, warm glow of light. It is closely related to *kagerou*, which is often rendered with the Chinese characters 陽 (sun) and 炎 (flame). The term *kagerou* expresses the beams of sunlight that flicker up in waves from the open fields on a spring day.

From a semantic standpoint, these two words—*kagiroi* and *kagerou*—are identical. In fact, any word containing *kagi*, *kage*, or even *kaga* or *kagu* evokes the same general physical phenomenon: light glimmering or flickering. *Kage*, for example, usually means *shadow*—but it can also mean the opposite: *light*. The *kage* of *tsukikage* denotes the moon's luminosity, not its shadow. The "Shining Princess" (*kagayaku o-himesama*) of the famous tenth-century fictional prose narrative *Taketori Monogatari* (*The Tale of the Bamboo Cutter*) is Princess Kaguya (Kaguya-hime); the *kagu* in her name denotes "shining," not darkness.

As far back as Book 1 of the *Man'yōshū*, we find a *waka* by the great poet Kakinomoto no Hitomaro (active late 7th c.) that includes the term *kagiroi*:

> Himugashi no   In the eastern fields
> no ni kagiroi no   the shimmering blaze [*kagiroi*]
> tatsu miete   can be seen rising

Kakinomoto's poem depicts the first light of dawn emerging over mountain crags as the sun begins to rise. Given that this *kagiroi* appears over the plain, however, this subtle phenomenon is completely different from the kind of open illumination that takes place at the first light of dawn (*akebono*).

かぎろひ

As the sun emerges over the mountain ridge, it not only releases powerful shafts of sunlight that appear to rise into the sky but also emits countless *kagiroi* over the great plain that stretches out before the poet's eye, flooding the entire scene in shimmering luminescence.

It is in this sense that *kagiroi* is synonymous with *kagerou.*

Kakinomoto composed his poem while he was living on the great plain, the sacred setting where Japanese people have worshiped the rising sun as a deity for centuries. At the foot of the hill is a Shinto shrine dedicated to the great deity (*kami*) of Ise Shrine: Amaterasu-ōmikami, the greatest deity in Shinto mythology and the divine incarnation of the sun.

To Kakinomoto, the great plain that stretched out before his eyes served as a canvas filled with the brilliant radiance of the divine sun deity Amaterasu-ōmikami, shining down from heaven.

We often hear how more than half the earth's population currently resides in urban areas. For city dwellers, it is nearly impossible to witness the sun make its natural ascent over the horizon.

That, I think, is why we need to cherish the sun's inimitable banquet of light all the more. Considering how difficult it is to behold the phenomenon of the sun's rising firsthand, witnessing the multicolored celebration of light emanating from the sun's wondrous arrival—even if only in our imaginations—is an experience to savor. My hope is that we forever continue to embrace the exquisitely beautiful term *kagiroi*, even if only as a thread that ties us into the realm of imagination.

Kagiroi

かぎろひ

Aburaderi

Oily Sun on a Sultry Day

buraderi refers to the scorching rays of sunlight that beat down ferociously on muggy days in midsummer—a phenomenon that many are surely familiar with.

There is perhaps no greater concern to humans than the issue of sunlight. Our concern only grows as we learn more and more about how harmful direct exposure to sunlight can be.

I recently read an article about how stores are now selling vast quantities of parasols designed exclusively for men, even.

As this boom in sun-protection products suggests, we tend to measure the sun's value by the single criterion of its physical benefit or detriment to us. This mentality troubles me.

The term *aburaderi*, however, gives me hope. Just hearing the word, I can't help but feel a deep sense of admiration.

My affection for the word stems from the connotations of *abura*, which means "oil" or "fat." Words that begin with *abura* abound. Take *aburanagi*, for instance, which denotes water at perfect stillness (*nagi*), appearing as though some thick, oily substance has been spread over it. *Aburazuki* refers to the smooth sheen of the moon (*tsuki*), so seemingly glossy that it looks as though someone has smothered oil all around it. The same goes for *aburazemi*, the cicada (*semi*) that sings all day long: *gee-gee-gee, gee-gee-gee*, ending with a click that sounds like hot oil popping.

The crown jewel of these *abura* words is no doubt the *aburamushi*, a particularly loathsome insect. This thoroughly unpleasant, intrusive bug that gnaws its

あぶらでり

way into every corner of your home without the slightest hesitation gets
its name not only from its awkward, almost greasy-looking body but also from
its distinctive uncleanliness—a quality more befitting a cockroach and one that
makes dealing with *aburamushi* as frustrating as dealing with kitchen grease.

The source of the second part of the term, *deri* or *teri* 照り, which denotes
sunshine, possesses many of the same connotations as *abura*. The kind of sunshine that feels as though you were being splashed with a thick, greasy-like
substance: this is almost unbearable. The word for this nasty grease-like *hideri*
sunshine that we experience on such hot sultry days is *aburaderi*.

When the heat is particularly scorching and the sun particularly blazing, even
a simple, off-hand exchange of mutual acknowledgment—"Boy, today sure is a
hot *aburaderi*" (*aburaderi desu ne*)—can ease the burden by showing us that, yes,
someone out there is in the same unpleasant predicament.

But then again, it is perhaps better that we experience this *aburaderi* in isolation. This sort of downright sweltering *aburaderi* heat does exist, to be sure, but
it is invariably accompanied by an occasional cool breeze that blows in. I suppose
the fact that we experience this sweltering heat and cool breeze in tandem adds
a kind of depth to our lives; indeed, this constant fluctuation from discomfort
to comfort and then back again might be said to be the very essence of life itself.
Surely this natural mode of life beats relying on air-conditioning and living in a
monotonous way, wouldn't you say?

Hoteri
■ Red Hot Flush

When rendered in Chinese characters, *hoteri* is a compound of "fire" (*hi* 火) and "sunshine" (*teri* 照).

The term is often used to describe the hot, red glow of a human face blushing from embarrassment, the palpable sensation of reddening cheeks.

The term, incidentally, also describes the red flush of the glowing sunset at dusk (*yūyake*). The poetry collection *Shinsen Rokujō Dai Waka* (compiled 13th c.) contains a *waka* that describes the blazing *hoteri* glow over the mountain edges, while boats of fishermen set sail with hopes of good weather for the following day. The depiction suggests that our forebears used the word *hoteri* to express the dusk-hour glow that would light up the entire ocean surface.

In the modern period, we find a similar depiction in a poem by the prominent poet Kitahara Hakushū,[9] who was active during the Taishō and early Shōwa periods. Prompted by feelings of nostalgia for his birthplace in Chikushi district, Fukuoka Prefecture, Hakushū wrote a collection of poems called *Kikyorai* (Returning Home), which included a poem containing the line: "the bay in the evening sun, stained red by the *hoteri* glow" (*hoteri shimu yūhi no kata*).

Hakushū's poem, in turn, recalls a much older poem from Book 1 of the *Man'yōshū*. Here, the poet anticipates tomorrow's full moon from the rays of the setting sun hovering above the sea and shining through a fleecy bank of clouds—what the premodern Japanese called *toyohata-gumo*. This appears to be the first instance of *hoteri* in a literary text.

This means that for over 1,300 years, countless Japanese poets have sung of this natural wonder called *hoteri*.

9. Kitahara Hakushū (1885–1942)

But how did this *hoteri* of the burning sunset go on to become the *hoteri* of a bashful countenance, that distinctive reddening? Might the sun grow similarly bashful at the way it has dyed the dusk sky above the sea a crimson red, thereby bringing the day to a close?

In Europe, artists generally depict the sun in shades of yellow. Some have even regarded the image of a sunflower or a dandelion as an actual sun. To the Japanese imagination, however, the sun is decidedly red.

Next time you observe the sun, note how it glows red in the morning and evening and yellow at midday. The Japanese seem to have instinctively regarded the image of the sun in the morning and evening as its most iconic. The Japanese sun, then, is the *hoteri* sun.

And why shouldn't it be? When Japanese people stare into the glare of the sun and squint their eyes, what do they see under their eyelids? Red.

And when we contemplate the sun in a spiritual way, isn't the sun that appears in our mind's eye a red one? For the Japanese, the *hoteri* sun is not so much the sun of the physical world as it is an abstraction: a sun that resides not only in nature but also within our meditating minds.

The *hoteri* that appears on the human face and the *hoteri* that appears in the setting sun are essentially the same. This bashfulness that comes over the young, innocent sun as it naïvely makes his morning ascent and disappears behind the evening horizon could very well be precisely what invites us to quiet contemplation.

Nonosama
The Moon as Law

People often classify *nonosama*, along with its close variant *nonnosama*, as children's words. To my mind, however, they are perfectly suitable for use by both children and adults. Indeed, I would love to hear *nonosama* more often in daily conversation.

Nonosama refers to the moon, which we often call *o-tsukisama*.

Why do we call the moon by the name *nonosama*? In fact, the term is an abbreviation of *nonnonsama*, which is the repetitive form of *nonsama*. True, repetition is a characteristic of children's words. Take *hai-hai*, for instance, which denotes the way babies crawl around on the floor. Or *o-chinchin*, which refers to a little boy's willy. There are countless other examples.

But what does *nonsama* mean, exactly? In classical antiquity, there was a government office called the Shikibushō Ministry, which was charged with regulating and enforcing laws. The office was also known as Nori no Tsukasa, or Law Bureau. Your average person on the street, however, pronounced it as Nonno Tsukasa. *Nori* became *non*, thereby making *nonsama* a derivation of *norisama*. *Nori* means the law.

That raises the question of why the moon would have associations with the law. Well, around the eighth century, our ancestors established a ceremony called the Yama no Nenbutsu (Amida contemplations), a week-long ceremony held at the foot of Mount Hiei in mid-autumn. At some point during that week, the mid-August harvest moon, or *chūshū no meigetsu*, would emerge. The long-standing custom of *o-tsukimi*, or moon viewing parties, also has its origins

のの
さ
ま

in this ancient ceremony. During the Yama no Nenbutsu, participants would turn their gazes toward the harvest moon and intone "Namu Amida Butsu"—"I take refuge in Amida Buddha"—whereupon the moon would instantaneously "transform" into the *norisama* of Buddhist law; they witnessed the *nori* moon of Buddhist law (*nori*). The light of that moon, therefore, shone with the "moonbeams of absolute truth" (*shin'nyo no tsuki*), as the Buddhist phrase has it.

The *nonsama* nickname, so rich in meaning, is one we Japanese people should embrace. Imagine a father, having spied the ascendant moon from his apartment window, saying to his child, "Look at how beautiful the *nonsama* is tonight." It's a heartening image, if I may say so.

And when the child asks him, "Daddy, why do we call the moon *nonsama*?" all he needs to say is, "Because that's what we called it when I was a kid." His child says, "No way!" and squeezes his father's hand as they gaze together at the moon.

Recently, I made a welcome discovery while quietly observing customers at a restaurant. To my surprise, I found that most diners still put their hands together as a gesture of gratitude before eating. This symbolic gesture seems especially noticeable among young women. The fact that they do it almost unconsciously makes it all the more endearing.

I, for one, am happy to know that the Japanese haven't given up on this practice just yet. It gives me hope that someday, maybe, we might revive the practice of calling the moon *nonosama*.

Nonosama

ののさま

Hanagumori

■ Cloudy Skies over Cherry Blossoms
in Full Bloom

*H*anagumori is written with the Chinese characters *hana* 花 (flower) and *kumori* 曇り (cloudy skies). The *hana* of *hanagumori* refers specifically to the cherry blossom (*sakura*). Combining the *sakura* blossoms with the image of *kumori*, the term expresses the cloudy skies that appear in early spring when cherry blossoms start to bloom in rich profusion.

Since the dawn of recorded history, the Japanese have attached great value to the cherry blossom. That devotion began long before the relatively new "Somei Yoshino" species of cherry tree—which is by far the most numerous species today—appeared in Japan in the Edo period. The tradition of cherry blossom viewing, or *hanami*, also dates back some 1,500 years to the time when the wild cherry tree (*yamazakura*) was the dominant species of cherry tree.

Cherry trees have an extremely short flowering span and fragile-looking petals. Japan's hazy spring climate is by no means temperate or clement, making the cherry blossom that much more ephemeral in nature. Spring weather tends to be rather unstable, marked by periodic heavy rains and fierce winds. In general, spring is the opposite of autumn, with its azure skies that stretch clear all the way up into the heavens.

Caught between two contradictory extremes—the evanescence of the cherry blossom and the volatile weather—Japanese people are rarely at ease during the spring season. Then again, perhaps it is precisely because the cherry blossoms exist under such precarious conditions that people's hearts are so restless. You might even say that the anxiety pervading springtime is what engenders such a loving attachment to cherry trees. Indeed, the human heart is unfathomable.

はなぐもり

Hanagumori is another expression of the season's contradictory character: layers of clouds spread out across the sky while cherry blossoms bloom wildly underneath. Rain may start to fall any moment now, it seems.

These expansive blankets of clouds in the early spring sometimes create apparitions of halos around the sun and the moon, making the scene even more melancholic.

The so-called *yozakura* custom of viewing the cherry blossoms at night under this halo-crowned, pale moon is a popular pastime—and the inspiration for many Nihonga, that popular Japanese style of modern painting that originated in the Meiji period, which often depicted the double image of the *yozakura* and the halo-ringed moon.

Hanagumori skies are the key ingredients behind that vague, spring-like atmosphere. For things to qualify as "spring-like," the sky must provide some contrast with a cloudy backdrop—bright blue skies would oversaturate the mood.

Years ago, I wrote a *tanka* poem that describes a cherry blossom tree shimmering brightly against a blazing sun in the background. But you could also describe the opposite: that, rather, the perfect stillness of mist-like cherry tree petals blooming in wild profusion and then blooming some more under the billowing layers of haze-trailing clouds constitutes a more fitting image for spring.

In that unmistakably indolent spring atmosphere, when our hearts seem to carry a twinge of "spring melancholy" (*shunshū*), *hanagumori* provides the perfect backlighting.

Tasogare

■ The Twilight Hour
(When One Distrusts Even a Friend)

T he time of day when we notice that evening (*yūgata*) has come is not the same time of day when we notice that *tasogare* (twilight hour) has come. Often translated as "twilight" or "dusk" or "the gloaming," *tasogare* refers to the time of day when our work is done and we deduce, intellectually, that evening (*yūgata*) is upon us—only to take a deep breath and intuit, perceiving the ineffable quality of the scenery outside, that it is now the *tasogare* hour.

Tasogare consists of three components: *ta* 誰 (who) + *so* そ (emphasis particle) + *kare* 彼 (he). You could translate it as "Who in the world is he?" or, more idiomatically, "Who's there?" In short, *tasogare* is the time of day when the sunlight has grown so dim that you can no longer discern who or what is there, leaving you to wonder—"Who goes there?" Centuries ago, the Japanese called this puzzling time of day *tasogare.*

People might recall that there is a similar story behind the opposite phenomenon of dawn (*yoake*)—and they are correct in making this connection. The word *kawatare* (twilight before dawn) simply switches the characters for *ta* (*tare*) and *kare* (*ka*): "he" (*ka* 彼) + "is" (*wa* は) + "who" (*tare* 誰), literally means, "He is who?" This term refers to the sliver of time just before dawn when it is still too dark outside to discern appearances. In short, *tasogare* and *kawatare* are identical in terms of substance: the same expressions, only inverted.

Interesting as these two terms may be, I couldn't help but wonder why our predecessors were so obsessed with identifying figures in the dim light. Where does that "who" (*dare* 誰) fixation come from?

But then I realized something. In peaceful times such as ours, people have little need to worry about who or what might be lurking out there in the dim light.

たそがれ

Such times, however, have been extremely rare over the entire course of human history. For most of that span, periods of constant caution and vigilance have been far more common than those of peace.

Then again, contemporary Japan is not without its own demons. When I was a kid, adults would warn us that kidnappers (*hitosarai*) were lurking around every corner, waiting in the shadows to whisk us away if we didn't hurry home after school. The sad fact is that abduction in Japan is worse now than it was then.

The *tasogare* hour is something that we perceive on a direct, physical level. The entire city landscape turns an opaque, yellowish color. For several minutes, the shapes of phenomena become unfixed and indeterminate, blurring into one another. Drivers on the road are keenly aware of how *tasogare* affects perception. This kind of sensory distortion can be explained in naturalistic, scientific terms, of course.

Even so, I marvel at the singular ability of the Japanese language to take the geophysical phenomenon of twilight and convert it to the psychological question "Who goes there?" (*Ta so gare?*), not to mention lend it widespread currency.

I can't help but feel a deep veneration toward this word *tasogare*, toward its moral implications. The word suggests an entirely different understanding of reality, a harsher view of the world far removed from our safe, everyday world that simply tells us to turn on the light when our room gets dark at night. When we act from the assumption that it is the hour when demons lurk, even old Kobutori Jiisan—literally "Boil-Removing Old Man"—might be lucky enough to get a demon to remove the boils from his face.

Ariake

■ Break of Day

Long ago, the moon and the sun had a nasty spat. From that point on, the two no longer spent their time together in the sky. The day was split into two halves: day and night.

Despite their separation, though, there remained a short span in each day when they could be together. The moon would carelessly forget her duty and belatedly make her ascent into the night sky, lingering on late into morning after the sun had risen, reluctant to reach her preordained destination under the western edge of the sky.

Night would turn to day, even as the moon still hung there lazily aloft in the sky. At some point, this remaining moon came to be called the "dawn moon," or *ariake no tsuki* (有明の月). It is called the *ariake* moon because the moon (*tsuki*) remains in the sky even after night has brightened (*ake*) into day. The *ari* part simply means the moon is still there, thus *ariake*. Generally, the moon we see hovering in the early morning sky around the twentieth day of the old lunar calendar is precisely this so-called "dawn moon."

As it happens, the full moon makes its ascent at just the right time of day on the fifteenth day of the old calendar, gracefully sweeping across the night sky with pinpoint timing. Its position then gradually shifts one night at a time: the *izayoi* (wafting) moon of the sixteenth night, the *tachimachi* (standing, waiting) moon of the seventeenth night, the *imachi* (sitting, waiting) moon of the eighteenth night, and then the *nemachi* (sleeping, waiting) moon of the nineteenth night.

After the twentieth day of each month, however, the moon cuts a rather gaunt, wasted figure in the morning sky. With the sun already in the sky, the moon is a *zangetsu*: a leftover, as it were, still slightly visible in a pale white hue.

The *ariake* "dawn moon" has an ashen, fragile look—and exudes an unbearably wistful emotional effect, which accounts for its popularity through the ages.

In classical times, male courtiers would make furtive visits to their lovers' bedchambers under cover of moonlight. It was customary for these men to leave their lovers in the early hours of the morning, when it was still dark outside, in order to avoid being seen. The moon under which these men stole away after dawn was, of course, that same "dawn moon."

The "dawn moon" is what greeted those courtly women who had sat up waiting anxiously for their lovers to arrive, only to welcome the morning alone.

Even in our modern world, we still catch occasional glimpses of that faint, leftover dawn moon visible in the morning, way up in the sky high above the tall buildings. The company employee, having stayed up all night working, might spy the pale, lingering moon in the dawn sky (*akatsuki*) hovering over the lonesome metropolis. Humanity's ongoing dialogue with the *zangetsu* moon will continue as long as we are still around. And each time this mutual communication takes place, I shall be reminded of that generations-old Japanese confection known as the *zangetsu* "leftover moon."

Ariake

ありあけ

Mugetsu
No Moon

In Japan, the moon on the fifteenth night of the eighth month of the old calendar—normally around September fifteenth in the modern calendar—is called the *chūshū no meigetsu*, or "mid-August harvest moon." Yet on this night, the clouds in the night sky are thicker than usual and the moon is nowhere to be seen.

The premodern Japanese came up with the name *mugetsu—mu* 無 (no, nothing) + *getsu* 月 (moon)—for this moon that remains unseen in the sky. They effectively brought the invisible mid-August harvest moon into existence by specifically christening it the *mugetsu*.

The notion of "no moon" came as a shocking discovery for me. Anglophones use the English word *nobody* in a similar sense to refer to the state of nobody present, as in "nobody there." The idea behind *mugetsu* follows a similar vein— and it's a rather un-Japanese mode of expression, a phrase that is atypical in the Japanese lexicon.

And yet, on the night of this mid-August "no moon," virtually everyone gazes upward and strains to see the moon anyhow. Peering into the sky, do we hold in our hearts an image of the full harvest moon (*meigetsu*)? And when we happen to find even a faint trace of what appears to be moonlight, do we not somehow feel that we have spotted the full harvest moon?

In short, the *mugetsu* somehow exists in a state of non-existence. It is being in non-being. It is the moon that both is and yet is not. The term *mugetsu* captures that phantasmagorical moon, a captivating contradiction.

Another close relative of the "no moon" idea is the term *ugetsu*, written

むげつ

with the Chinese characters *u* 雨 (rain) and *getsu* 月 (moon). This *ugetsu* also evokes the notion of the full *meigetsu* moon hidden behind the clouds on a rainy mid-autumn night. In the same way as *mugetsu*, *ugetsu* is a moon that was imagined as a hallucination over the rainclouds, and a phantasmagorical moon that shines only inside human hearts and minds.

Haiku poetry prizes the elegance of bringing things into existence by enunciating absence, nothingness. Here's a haiku by one of Matsuo Bashō's[10] followers, Ochi Etsujin:[11]

Ame no tsuki	Moon on a rainy night
doko to mo nashi no	emanating from nowhere
usuakari	the dim light.

A modern haiku that illustrates my point is the following poem by Shida Sokin[12] from the collection *Yamahagi* (Bush Clover):

Santō ya	Range of mountains—
mugetsu no sora no	in the moonless sky
soko akari	an illusory glow.

The dim light (*usuakari*) of the first haiku and the illusory glow (*sokoakari*) of the second haiku both express moonlight faintly floating up in in the poets' hearts.

10. See note 2 on page 301   11. Ochi Etsujin (1656–ca. 1739)   12. Shida Sokin (1876–1946)

Akebono

Dim Twilight of the Dawn

There are several ways to express *dawn* in Japanese. The simplest way is *yoake*, which literally means "night turning bright." This term is written with the Chinese characters "night" (*yo* 夜) and "to brighten" (*ake* 明け). Another way is *asa-ake*, which denotes morning (*asa*), or the point when night has brightened (*ake*) into day. It can be rather disconcerting when you picture *morning* brightening (*asa ga akeru*) when, in fact, what brightens is the night: *yo ga akeru*.

Another term for dawn is *akebono*. This refers to the time when night turns to day, ever so faintly, in an ever so *honobono* way. Accordingly, *akebono* is sometimes called *honobono-ake*. Every Japanese person knows that the Chinese character for *akebono* is 曙.

There is a subtle—but vital—distinction between *akebono* and *yoake*, however. As I see it, the adverb *honobono* expresses the way the sunlight shines at this time of day. The morning sun, or *asahi*, releases shafts of light into the earth's atmosphere. The outward appearance of this natural phenomenon is what we call *akebono*. That's how I understand it, at least.

That representation informed the design for the Rising Sun Flag of Japan and, in turn, became the trademark for several famous Japanese companies. It even appeared on the label for a certain canned salmon product: the famous Akebono salmon. Regardless of the context, the word *akebono* always means that the sun is rising.

Yoake, by contrast, denotes the simple passage of time from night to dawn. It

あけぼの

is therefore altogether different from *akebono* in terms of overall feeling.

Honobono, which lies at the heart of the notion of *akebono*, is an example of a mimetic word. The term seems to have originated in the adjective *honoka* (*na*), meaning "faint," but it eventually came to be identical with *bonyari*, another mimetic word that suggests faintness in appearance. It follows, then, that the temporal point of *yoake* likely emerged from the general feeling evoked by a particular state of the sky, which was then developed into a concept. This method of devising new Japanese words strikes me as original and ingenious.

For over a thousand years, Japanese people have treasured a certain distinguished literary work that begins with this mimetic word *akebono*. I'm thinking of that collection of essays that begins with the famous opening sentence: "Spring is dawn" (*haru wa akebono*), which might be paraphrased as "The best thing about spring is its dawn." The work is *Makura no Sōshi* (*The Pillow Book*), written around 1002.

The author of this work, Sei Shōnagon,[13] was a lady-in-waiting in the imperial court who despised glibness for its own sake. The book evinces that taste, with its simple, terse statement about how *akebono* dawns are the hallmark of spring, leading off the work. She is right, too: the general feeling of faintness (*honobono*) is, in fact, a quality wholly unique to spring, not to be found in any other season. This description was especially apt for the hazy atmosphere in the capital city of Heian, modern-day Kyoto, where she lived. I can think of no better way to express it.

---

13. Sei Shōnagon (ca. 966–ca.1025)

Akebono

あけぼの

Kaminari
Thunder and Lightning

The sky turns ominously dark. Thunder echoes in the distance. This rumbling sound, or *kaminari* in Japanese, is said to be caused by a deity, or *kamisama*. This is the idea behind the origin of the term *kaminari*, which is written with the Chinese characters *kami* 神 (deity) and *nari* 鳴り (to sound).

Those who have done some reading in classical antiquity will know that the premodern Japanese feared nothing more than Raijin 雷神, the thunder deity. It was only after humans became steeped in civilization that they made the sun the king of all deities.

The thunder deity was regarded as chief deity not simply because of its power to instill fear through use of thunder and lightning, however. As is true in so many cases, the value of a thing is dependent on its usefulness to humans. Thus, the deity of thunder and lightning (*kaminari*) attained the status of supreme deity on account of its considerable contributions to agricultural production. As I explain in the entry for *inazuma* (see page 56), lightning played a major role in providing bountiful harvests and ensuring fertility for ancient communities.

Japanese has another word for lightning: *ikazuchi*. The word is a combination of two Chinese characters, 厳 (*ika*; august, majestic) and 霊 (*chi*; spirit, soul), and thus carries the connotation of "an august or majestic spirit." Lacking any determinate characteristics, the term referred simply to any kind of majestic or august spirit. In short, the word *ikazuchi* connotes the sense of awe that humans felt in the presence of the divine *kaminari* phenomenon.

Lightning divination, or *denkō uranai*, was a common practice throughout the ancient world. The widespread use of lightning in divination rituals testifies to the lightning god Raijin's importance and paramount status among the

myriad deities. Lightning divination was used to determine which god was in a state of rage by tracking the lightning's location in the sky. Once people had determined its source, they would give offerings to whichever god had released the lightning, in the hope of appeasing it.

There is another synonym for *kaminari*, and that is *kamutoke*. This term comes from the phenomenon of lightning—that massive cluster of divinity (*shintai*)—that occasionally thunders high in the heavens without revealing itself, instead just releasing occasional shafts of light. At times, the divine cluster experiences a dissolution of energy, which results in *kamutoke*—literally the "dissolution of a deity"—and from that heavenly breakdown come bolts of light, or *inazuma*.

Given the many Japanese words for expressing the phenomenon of *kaminari*, we can see that the premodern Japanese possessed a rather sophisticated understanding of what that divine cluster of energy signified.

Framed by this group of terms, lightning has long been revered as a "deity of the firmament" (*tenjō no kami*). In Japan, the deity known as Kamo evidently manifests itself as the deity of thunder. Most people today are familiar with the Wind God and Thunder God screens (*fūjin raijin zu*), which were popular during the Edo period. Whichever word we take—*kaminari*, *ikazuchi*, or *kamutoke*—they all echo the religious sense of awe and reverence that our forebears felt for the natural phenomenon of lightning and thunder.

The word *kaminari* possesses an uncanny, terrifying resonance, but it also suggests the deep feeling of kinship that we Japanese people have long sustained toward this natural phenomenon.

Inazuma
Bolts of Lightning

Everyone knows that *inazuma* 稲妻 refers to the fearsome shock of light that flashes through the vast vault of heaven. Very few people, however, have considered why this electrical bolt in the sky is called *ina + tsuma*: literally, "wife" (*tsuma* 妻) of "rice" (*ine* 稲).

Or perhaps some have indeed pondered this only to dismiss it as a curious oddity.

The fact of the matter, however, is that the term has rather profound implications.

To begin with, the *tsuma* of *inazuma* refers to *husband*. Originally, *tsuma* meant not "wife" (as it does today) but rather "one's partner." Thus, in the past, both husband and wife were called *tsuma*. Furthermore, we know from the records that the *tsuma* of *inazuma* meant "husband" rather than "wife."

So why do we call lightning the "husband" of "rice" (*ine*)? The answer is quite interesting. When a flash of *inazuma* runs through the sky, the nitrogen dissolves in midair and becomes nitrogenous fertilizer in the ground. In this way, the lightning *inseminates* the planted rice. Lightning is the "husband" of the rice, as it were.

The term *inazuma* appears in the *Kokin Wakashū*.[14] Before that, a similar, more primitive term was used in the *Nihon Shoki*,[15] namely, *inatsurubi*, which is written with the Chinese characters for "lightning" 雷 and "electricity" 電. *Inatsurubi* is a more direct expression signifying the sexual intercourse that takes place between lightning (*rai*) and rice (*ine*).

To put it more precisely: the idea behind the term is that the descent of

---

14. *Kokin Wakashū* (A Collection of Poems Ancient and Modern, ca. 905)
15. *Nihon Shoki* (The Chronicles of Japan, 720)

いなづま

lightning causes the mythical Emperor of Heaven, or *tentei* 天帝, to copulate with Jiten, the earth goddess. Their union thus bestows agricultural fertility on humankind.

There used to be a law forbidding people—even the "son of heaven," *tenshi*, the emperor—from engaging in sexual activity during a *kaminari* thunderstorm. Nevertheless, the *Nihon Ryōiki*,[16] one of Japan's oldest sources, includes a story that describes one case of an emperor breaking this commandment. When a servant inadvertently walks in on the emperor and empress making love during a thunderstorm, the enraged emperor commands the servant to "go seize the lightning and bring it hither at once!" (*Rai o toraete koi!*). The location in the city of Asuka where he managed to catch a lightning bolt later came to be known as Lightning Hill (*ikazuchi no oka*).

What I find astonishing is the precision with which the premodern Japanese were able to observe nature and respond to its workings accordingly. *Inazuma* is just one of the many examples of how they understood the natural world with such clarity.

Modern man, on the other hand, has only recently learned of the connection between lightning and agricultural production through explorations in mushroom cultivation. When it comes to the natural sciences, our predecessors might have had a better grasp of the facts than we do.

There may very well be other words that, like *inazuma*, reveal premodern Japanese people's intuitive understanding of nature. Even natural scientists might benefit from a closer reading of the classics.

16. *Nihon Ryōiki* (Record of Miraculous Events in Japan, compiled ca. 787–824)

Yukimoyoi
Signs of Imminent Snow

The word *yukimoyoi* scarcely exists in our contemporary language, but I'd like to see if I can't revive it. The word refers to the overcast winter skies that look as if it is just about ready to snow.

First, a short explanation about why this phenomenon is called *yukimoyoi* is in order.

Moyoi no doubt originated from the verb *moyou*, which does not appear anywhere in classical literature. The related verb *moyohosu* (催), however, does appear—rather frequently, in fact. Insofar as the verb *moyohosu* did exist, *moyou* was its prototype.

Another related term is *moyau*, a common archaic word. The Chinese character for the term was 舫, which means to drop anchor and moor a ship.

We can locate *moyou* in the same vicinity. *Moyohosu*, in the modern vernacular, carries the meaning "to hold a ceremony or function"—but its original meaning describes the point before that stage, the planning and preparation of a function. *Moyoosu* and *moyau* most likely referred to the preparation more than the actual execution. Even today, we use the verb *moyoosu* to describe the sensation of having to urinate, the anticipation of the act. *Moyai* 舫い (mooring a boat), too, suggests the preparation for setting sail.

Yukimoyoi skies are those distinctive skies that seem ready to release snow at any moment: snow about to burst forth naturally as if someone had prepared it

ゆきもよひ

for earthward descent.

The Japanese-Portuguese Dictionary *Vocabvlario da Lingoa de Iapam* (*Nippo Jisho*) was compiled by a Jesuit missionary in 1603 and includes Japanese terms in use in the late Muromachi period, including the phrase *shinjin o moyoosu*, which means "to put forth a devout heart." *Moyoosu* seems to have been an expression that attached great weight to the natural progression of things.

Having entertained my somewhat fanciful conjectures about the verb *moyou*, now imagine the night sky in Japan's northern regions in winter—you will immediately be struck by just how perfectly the term *yukimoyoi* describes these northerly winter skies.

At last, the snow starts to fall and then persists, without pause, for several more days. The townscape is a microcosm of wintry mountain country: the snow slowly starts to pile up, each snow-capped rooftop a miniature mountain peak, the village transforming into an expansive white terrain.

Small lamplights flicker on in windows, bringing scenes of *yukihotaru*—literally "fireflies in the snow"—to life. It was in that sort of home that eminent modern poet Miyoshi Tatsuji[17] in his poem "Snow" envisioned Tarō and Jirō going to sleep, with their mother quietly working beside them deep into the night.

17. Miyoshi Tatsuji (1900–1964)

Yukimoyoi

ゆきもよい

Kazahana

∎ Light Flurries

Kazahana is written with two Chinese characters: *kaze* 風 (wind) and *hana* 花 (flower). In fact, the word means something like "light snow-fall" (*koyuki*).

Kazahana was one of the first words that I acquired *unnaturally*, outside the course of everyday experience. I learned the word at a very young age from my late father, an amateur haiku poet. He often taught me various haiku terms, and one of them was *kazahana*. Even now, I distinctly remember being deeply moved by the word's beautiful resonance.

By "deeply moved," I mean the distinct sensation of having the word radiate before me in a kind of sublime light.

When I was much older, I came to realize that the word *kazahana* actually made frequent appearances in everyday conversations. Sometime in early winter, I noticed something fluttering in midair: tiny white flakes that resembled snow but were not quite full-fledged snow.

When someone says, "Oh, look, it's snowing," people often respond, "You're right—*kazahana*." That exchange, a rather common conversation, is a kind of mutual verification that winter has just begun.

The *kaza* of *kazahana* refers to the cold winds, or *samukaze*, that herald the arrival of winter. *Hana* means "nose" when written with the Chinese character 鼻, and, by extension, "vanguard" or "harbinger." Is *kazahana* the "harbinger" of cold winter winds, then? *Hana* can also mean "flower" when written with the Chinese character 花. Are the flurries "flower" petals, carried by the wind? Does the wind itself transform into a flurry of flowers, soon to fall and scatter on the ground? The image is a rather beautiful one, I must say.

Examples of snow being likened to flowers are found throughout Japa-

nese classical literature, even as far back as the eighth century. In Book 5 of the *Man'yōshū*, we find the following *waka*:

Waga sono ni   In my garden
ume no hana chiru   the plum blossoms fall—
hisakata no   or is it snow flowing
ame yori yuki no   from the distant heavens?
nagarekuru kamo

Ōtomo no Tabito[18]

The poem movingly depicts the falling and scattering of plum blossoms as the flowing snow. Even by the high standards of the *Man'yōshū*—which abounds with outstanding poems—the work is a *waka* masterpiece.

To be sure, the conceits of likening snow to flowers in the wind and likening flowers in the wind to snow are not the same. In both cases, however, the joining of the two images—snow descending through the sky and blossoms scattered on the ground—through the figurative medium of the wind is a splendid notion.

While we're on the subject, allow me to mention one additional phrase: *kikushiri no hana*. It refers to the "flower" (*hana*) that "blooms" after autumn's last blooming flower, the chrysanthemum (*kiku*). This "flower" appears just when you think the flower-blossoming season is over—and then, voilà, one more appears: snow. Here, too, the metaphor compares snow to a flower, and what a beautiful one it is.

---

18. Ōtomo no Tabito (665–731)

Kazahana

かざはな

Isaribi

■ Fish-luring Fires at Night

On the ocean surface at night, the fishing lamps flicker, dotting the scene here and there in a moving pattern. For many Japanese, the sight brings back memories with deep nostalgia.

These flickering lamps on fishing boats are called *isaribi*. The word is written with the Chinese characters *isari* 漁り (fishing) + *hi* 火 (fire, light).

The fishing lamps often feature prominently in aerial photographs of the Japanese nightscape. You could even say the boat lights are an emblem of the country.

This verb *isaru* (the verb form of *isari*), meaning "to fish," happens to be the same word etymologically as *asaru*, which means "to forage." You may be disappointed to learn that *isaru* and *asaru* share the same origins—but that relationship highlights an excellent side of the Japanese language, which draws a distinction between animals that forage (*asaru*) for sources of food and humans who fish (*isaru*) for their prey.

I remember feeling crestfallen after reading a poem by Kaneko Misuzu[19] called "Tairyō" (Big Catch), which describes humans celebrating a great haul while the surviving fish are conducting funeral rites. The awareness that the enterprise of fishing invariably goes hand in hand with the death of countless fish comes through in the word *isaru*, but the word *asaru* lacks that dimension.

When it comes to *isaribi*, I immediately imagine a squid fishing boat in the night.

---

19. Kaneko Misuzu (1903–1930)

A few years back, I stayed at an inexpensive traditional Japanese lodge in a town near the Sea of Japan. That night, the proprietress served me an *o-nabe* hot pot dish. While I was helping myself to the food with chopsticks, she set into relating her life story to me.

"My husband was a fisherman on a squid boat," she began. "But one night, he fell into the water and drowned. After that, I managed to make ends meet running this little lodge, all the while raising my son by myself. I didn't want my son to suffer the same fate, so I did what I could to get him through high school. I kept praying that he'd find a white-collar office job somewhere. But one day, he came home and announced that he wanted to follow in his old man's footsteps. He wouldn't listen to me. Now, he's left home to train to be a fisherman."

Her feelings are natural, to be sure, but her son's sentiments make sense, too. This confusing thing called life—*jinsei* in Japanese—will no doubt go on spinning its patterns out of this mess called life force—*inochi* in Japanese—one misthread at a time.

Since that night, whenever I see an *isaribi* out in the ocean, I immediately recall the image of that sad woman's wrinkled hands. In a way, the fishing-boat lights, blinking sadly in the sea, glinting here and there amid the lonely darkness of night, seem like the faint light emanating from us weak, fragile humans. We can no doubt trace the beauty of this word *isaribi* to that perception as well.

Kogarashi

Cold Late-Autumn Winds

Kogarashi denotes cold, harsh, tree-withering winds.

In haiku, *kogarashi* is a seasonal word—*kigo*—that falls into the winter category. But the term refers to the chilling winds that start to blow around late autumn and continue just until the start of winter.

The cold winds and rain that straddle these two seasons, like the winds and rain that come during the *shigure* rainy season (see page 88), have a kind of nebulous character that makes them hard to classify as either belonging to autumn or winter. They essentially bridge the transition from one season to the next, in a slow, gradual pattern.

The chill in the air grows colder each day, starting around the end of autumn. The sky grows thick with heavy clouds; in the morning, you start wondering whether it might be time to start bundling up in warmer clothes. When you awake, you notice the trees starting to turn yellow and red, their leaves numb from the cold.

At this point, the wind known as the *kogarashi*—which is written *ki* 木 (tree)+ *karashi* 枯らし (wither, die)—makes its appearance, blowing in with a cold gust, turning the trees bare and sparing not a single leaf. Of course, trees shed their leaves as a kind of defense mechanism that preserves the life of the tree; technically, then, a tree losing its leaves is not actually withering away.

To my mind, a beautiful word is one that gracefully bridges the gap between objective fact and subjective human impression. If *kogarashi* denoted a wind so brutal that it actually *did* cause the trees to die off completely, the word would evoke no lyrical impressions. The fact that the natural *kogarashi* phenomenon doesn't kill the trees is what gives the word its poetic quality—a dimension

こ
が
ら
し

that makes *kogarashi* a fitting name for literary characters. Take assassin Kogarashi Monjirō, for instance, the main character of Sasazawa Saho's eponymous novel, which Ichikawa Kon made into a TV series in 1972–1973. By contrast, the decidedly unlyrical pine wood nematode (*matsukui mushi*), which actually does wither and kill pine trees, will always have a hard time finding its way into the names of fictional characters.

I am also quite fond of the related word *kōraku*, a combination of the Chinese characters for "yellow" 黄 and "falling" 落, which describes the landscape that the *kogarashi* winds leave in their wake: tree leaves turn yellow and fall, the larger ones piling atop one another on the ground, forming a heap that makes a crackling sound—the very sound of winter.

A superb haiku about the *kogarashi* winds from the Edo period goes:

Kogarashi no	Tree-withering gust
hate wa arikeri	reaching its ultimate end:
umi no oto	sound of the ocean.
	Ikenishi Gonsui [20]

As the poem suggests, the writer hears the booming sound of the tide (*shionari*) after the *kogarashi* winds sweep through (although the "sound of the ocean" he refers to is, in fact, Lake Biwa). The *kogarashi* winds enter the sea, only to transform into the roaring tide.

This grand, circular movement—an eternal return—is the life force of nature.

---

20. Ikenishi Gonsui (1650–1722)

Ikanobori

Squid-shaped Paper Flying Kite

*I*kanobori and *tako* basically refer to the same thing: traditional Japanese flying kites.

The history of the kite in Japan is quite long. The concept seems to have been imported from China as early as the tenth century—but it wasn't until the Edo period that it acquired the meaning it currently has today for Japanese people: the fish-shaped kites that we see swimming up there, high in the sky, riding the wind.

According to one theory, the objects are called *tako* (octopus) in the Kantō region (eastern Japan) and *ika* (squid) in the Kansai (western) and Hokuriku (northwestern) regions. We know that by the tenth century, Japanese people had already begun cutting paper in the shape of *tobi*, or "kite bird" in English. And so, when the flying kite changed from airborne bird to a sea creature at some point, it became *tako* in the east and *ika* in the west.

Both *tako* and *ika* got their names from imagining creatures with tails attached. From the standpoint of the formation of Japanese culture, the fact that east Japan and west Japan use different terms—*tako* and *ika*—for the same form of recreation is of great interest. The object used by Benjamin Franklin in his experiments was also a *tako*, which happens to be called "kite" (also taking its name from the "kite bird") in English.

I grew up in the eastern Kantō region, so I always called the kite by the name *tako*, or "octopus." At some point, however, I encountered this other word—*ikanobori*—and immediately took to it.

It wasn't so much that the word *ikanobori* itself was anything special; rather, it

いかのぼり

was that it made a notable appearance in the following magnificent haiku by Yosa Buson:[21]

Ikanobori	Paper kite
kinō no sora no	in the same place as it was
aridokoro	in yesterday's sky.

Here, the poet is gazing up at a vacant sky; all he sees there is empty space, or what is called "absolute emptiness" (*kokū*) in Buddhism. And yet, in that empty sky, Buson can still make out the spectral vision of a kite that had been flying there just yesterday, an image that had seared itself in his mind's eye. The kite stays there, fixed for all eternity, never making even the slightest flutter.

The kite in Buson's haiku, then, stands for all things of this world that exist amid absolute emptiness, that leave remnant traces even after they have vanished. It is this symbolic resonance that pervades the term *tako* that moves us so deeply.

There is a more recent poem called "Tako" (Kite) by Nakamura Minoru (b. 1927), and the beautiful verse describes the kite in a similar way. Though the kite appears to be perfectly still, Nakamura writes, it flutters continuously in the wind. I suppose Yosa Buson, too, saw the same deceptive stillness that Nakamura's kite evokes, an analog for our own moving—yet somehow static—lives. Ever since I encountered these two poems, *ikanobori* has become a truly magical word to me.

21. Yosa Buson (1716–1784)

Ironaki Kaze

■ Colorless Wind

In Chinese philosophy, there is a system of thought called *gogyō shisō*, which might be translated as the "five phases." According to this system, each of the four seasons is assigned a specific color: spring is blue, summer vermillion, autumn white, and winter the deep black expressed by the Chinese character *gen* 玄.

The Chinese word *hakushū* 白秋—"white autumn"—was born from the notion that autumn is white. The renowned modern poet Kitahara Hakushū made his debut in the literary world after taking *Hakushū* for his pen name. Matsuo Bashō's great *haibun* work *Oku no Hosomichi* (*The Narrow Road to the Deep North*) also contains a famous haiku that describes autumn as white:

Ishiyama no	Even whiter than
ishi yori shiroshi	the stones of stone mountain:
aki no kaze	autumn's wind.

Bashō thus renders autumn wind (*aki no kaze*) as a white wind, echoing the *gogyō shisō* framework. In the poem, the whiteness of the wind is even more perfect and pristine than the white face of a stony mountain.

There is another phrase, however, that equates the autumn wind (*aki no kaze*) not with the color white but rather with the absence of all color: *ironaki kaze*, or "colorless wind." The phrase is identical in meaning to the *so* of the term *sofū* 素風, which denotes autumn wind with the added connotation of absence or insignificance.

The very idea of the "white wind" color interpretation in the *gogyō* tradition is rich and captivating enough on its own, but the term takes on a stunningly novel, boldly expressive seasonal dynamic when you conceive the wind as *ironaki kaze*, one devoid of color altogether. There is a haiku by the contemporary poet Fukuda Takao that goes:

Tsuribashi o	In colorless wind
wataru ironaki	that crosses over
kaze no naka	the hanging bridge

The poem puts the reader within a moving, colorless, transparent wind, fully exposed to the center of the universe.

The brisk feeling caused by this "colorless" autumn wind is also accompanied by its opposite: a twinge of melancholy. The gradual change into autumn beckons humanity into a place of quiet, meditative contemplation. The transparency of that colorless wind would never be conceivable in any season but autumn.

いろなきかぜ

Nowaki
▪ Strong Winds in Autumn

In Japan, the autumn season invariably brings with it a series of powerful typhoons, which make landfall in quick succession. The most typical of these typhoons comes around the 210th day of the year.

By "210th day of the year," I mean the 210th day in the old lunar calendar, which was used in Japan until the Meiji period. This calendar counted the days starting from the first day of spring, or *risshun*, which falls on February 4th in the modern calendar. Therefore, in the old calendar, the 210th day refers to the time around the start of the ninth lunar month—a time when powerful winds would blow right on a fixed schedule, as if to remind us that we'd once again made it to the 210th day.

The premodern Japanese coined a term for the fierce autumn winds: *nowaki*. Today, *nowaki* is more commonly pronounced *nowake*. Natsume Sōseki,[22] the great Meiji-period novelist, effectively established this old word as a modern term when he used it for the title of his novel *Nowaki* (1907).

Whether we pronounce these two characters—野 (*no*; plain) and 分 (*wake*, *waki*; cutting or tearing through)—as *nowake* or *nowaki*, the word clearly gets its name from strong autumn gales tearing through the plains, leveling all the grass in their wake. The verb *wakeru* means "to separate" or, in this context, "to tear through something."

Interestingly, there is a related term, *moromuki*, which expresses the state of grass bending in all directions. The term appears as far back as the *Man'yōshū* (Book 14). Evoking the image of blades of grass knocked down "this way and that way" (*moromuki*) by the force of the wind, the term gives us a glimpse into the vast breadth of the Musashino Plain.

---

22. Natsume Sōseki (1867–1916)

The premodern Japanese were obviously acutely aware of how the wind moved—and that cognizance is precisely what produced the word *nowaki*. After all, the directional course of the wind determines the angle at which the grasses fall.

Thus, we have *nowaki*, written *no* 野 (fields) + *wake* 分け (divide). The wind essentially cleaves the grasses into various directions on the plain. Our forebears went beyond simply noticing the wind's power as it swept across the fields; they also paid close attention to the pathways that those rough gusts traveled.

Even today, we can see the same phenomenon when we survey the rice paddies after violent storm winds have blown through: we find the poor little rice stalks pitifully levelled, bending in all directions. The wind leaves scars as it blows round and round, wreaking so much havoc that it's easy to imagine the arduous task of the poor farmer who has to clean things up in the field. The rice is brutally pounded "this way and that way" (*moromuki*) at the mercy of the wind. The ravaged scene is the essence of the *nowaki* nuance.

Still, the rough, uninhibited *nowaki* winds are not merely a malevolent force. If you observe the aftermath the day after the winds have died down, you can see how the *nowaki* gusts have also blown the leaves from the trees onto the lattices of every door, almost as if they placed them there purposefully. That very impression even appears in Sei Shōnagon's celebrated work, *Makura no Sōshi*.

On the one hand, the great *nowaki* winds put on a violent show that seems capable of cutting the field into pieces. And yet these same winds, incredibly, are also capable of weaving delicate, intricate designs. Since antiquity, Japanese people have embraced both sides of this natural phenomenon, the "*nowaki* winds."

Wakamizu

■ "Young Water" Drawn on the Morning of
New Year's Day

The first water drawn on the first morning of the New Year is called *waka-mizu,* which literally means "young water."

When I was a child, most households still got their water from either the tap or a well with a manual pump that drew the water out from underground.

In those days, it was a custom on New Year's Day to get a quick bucket of water from the well in the lingering dark before the break of dawn. My parents would wake me up and say, "Head out to the well and draw a cup of *wakamizu!*" Why did they call that first-drawn water on New Year's Day "young water?" It was a question that stuck with me, child as I was. I wondered how on earth water could have an age—how water could be youthful or elderly.

As I grew older, though, the question slowly resolved itself. Or rather, I slowly came to intuit the term's meaning in a physical sense. At that pure first dawn, the water, too, would greet the New Year and take on a fresh youthfulness, brimming with vitality.

And yet, conversely, water also grows old, tired, and worn, just as humans do as the days and months pile up. Unlike the water drawn on the morning of New Year's Day, the water drawn on New Year's Eve is world-weary and exhausted.

The premise behind this idea—that the New Year marks a radical break between death and rejuvenation—is of course the traditional *kazoedoshi* system of counting years in East Asia. According to this method, a person adds one

year to his life each time the calendar year changes. The "youthful" zest of New Year's water certainly doesn't well up so powerfully under the modern system of counting "completed years," or *mannenrei*, as opposed to the New Year-centric *kazoedoshi* method.

But even if we continue to reckon our age years according to the prevailing *mannenrei* style, we should still stay attuned to the idea of a mysterious life force that seems to renew itself from year to year.

By doing so, we will then naturally come to understand that water too possesses a kind of life, which grows older with each passing year; and so it is worth considering why New Year's water is regarded as "young."

When Japanese people first came up with this word, they believed that drinking the youngest of all water would grant them a dewy, youthful life.

Wakamizu is indeed a wonderful word, one that evokes a sense of cleanliness and dignity.

When I was a child, we'd first offer *wakamizu* at the household Shinto altar (*kamidana*) and Buddhist altar (*butsudan*); then, everyone would drink it in communion. Before you dismiss these practices as obsolete in the modern world, where we don't draw water from wells any more, remember that tap water works just as well. And, the next time the Japanese New Year (*shōgatsu* 正月) rolls around—ring in the occasion by enjoying a cup of "young water."

O-mizutori

■ Drawing Sacred Water

There is a Buddhist festival called the *shuni-e*. One of the most famous *shuni-e* occurs each year in the Nigatsu-dō—literally, the "second month hall"—at Tōdaiji, the famous temple in the ancient capital of Nara. As the names suggests—*shuni-e* literally means "second-month service"—the festival, an event to pray for the prosperity of the nation, was traditionally held in the second month of the old lunar calendar. But these days, it is held in March.[23]

Among the *shuni-e* rites is *o-mizutori*, which literally means "drawing sacred water." The event begins on March thirteenth, in the ealy hours before dawn. Participants draw water from the *wakasa-i*, the "well of Wakasa province," next to the Nigatsu-dō and then offer it to the bodhisattva Guanyin, or Kannon in Japanese.

The water is said to come from the Hokuriku region, specifically, the former Wakasa province, now the southwestern portion of Fukui Prefecture. The distance from old Wakasa to Nara is over a hundred kilometers.

When people first hear that theory, they cannot believe their ears. Some dismiss it as a silly rumor. Others say it sounds like a quaint legend. I, too, found it hard to believe when I first heard it.

But there is, in fact, another ceremony that takes place in Wakasa on March second. This ceremony is known as the *o-mizuokuri*, which literally means "sending forth sacred water." I once saw it performed: in the bone-chilling cold of midnight, a crowd of people, some dressed in the robes of Buddhist priests,

---

23. A change that reflects Japan's adoption of the Gregorian calendar in 1872

others looking like mountain ascetics, started to gather; then, after offering their service prayers known as *butsuzen no ekō,* they sent the sacred water down the shallow rapids of a river known as the *u no se* (cormorant rapids) and off to the Nigatsu-dō far away in Nara.

Among the participants were laypersons as well, who brandished the pine torches called *taimatsu* and journeyed to the *u no se* to partake in the evening ritual alongside the priests and mountain ascetics. The event continued through the night, until the first traces of pale dawn announced its end.

Whenever I think of that ritual, I imagine some great water vein cutting across the earth from Wakasa to the old Yamato province, the site of the ancient capital of Nara—a massive subterranean conduit laid down underground over time.

Then again, the fantastical image of an underground water connection stretching over a lengthy expanse strikes me as a reflection of the homeland ideal. At one end, the sacred water is sent down the river. At the other end, the water is received. This exchange symbolizes the living breath of our native soil, which is permeated by an ever-youthful life force.

Indeed, the word itself—*o-mizutori*—stirs up thoughts of love for one's homeland. It carries an exquisite resonance. Each time I sound out its five syllables, I can picture the great underground stream flowing through the night, from Wakasa in the northwest down to the old Yamato province in the west, bound for the ancient capital of Nara.

Usurahi

Thin Coat of Ice

If you ever stop by downtown Asuka, Nara Prefecture, you will find a legendary spot on which stood an imperial palace from the Asuka period. The site held the seat of several imperial reigns in the latter half of the seventh century—the period between the reigns of Emperor Jomei[24] and Emperor Tenmu[25]—albeit with some interruptions.

The site also hosts a particularly famous well. At present, the original well has been refilled, but a replica of the original well has been built at the corresponding spot. Today, the location bustles with tourists.

When this well was discovered some thirty years ago, I happened to be staying at the nearby Tachibana Temple. I had heard the news of the discovery on the nightly news, so the first thing I did the next morning was rush to the excavation sight to see the finding for myself.

There, I found the well right before me, the surface of the water revealing itself after remaining hidden for over a millennium. It was totally covered with thin ice—*usui kōri* in Japanese. The old word for this sort of thin ice coating is *usurahi*, which is also written with the two Chinese characters *usui* 薄 (thin) and *kōri / hi* 氷 (ice). As soon as I saw the layer of ice on the well water, that ancient word—*usurahi*—immediately sprang to my mind. "It's *usurahi*!" I murmured to myself.

Since that day, whenever I think of the word *usurahi*, I always recall that scene I witnessed at the temple—largely because the experience itself was such a moving one, to be sure. But needless to say, I cannot forget the expressiveness of the thin coating of ice I saw, a sign that seemed to announce the arrival of winter. Though seemingly thin and precarious, the *usurahi* spread out in a fine layer that was resilient and stark.

When I was a kid, *usurahi* would often form on the surface of the *mizugame*

---

24. Emperor Jomei (ca. 593–641)   25. Emperor Tenmu (ca. 631–686)

(a big water jar) that sat outside our entryway. The *usurahi* ice would break apart as soon as I touched it. It was the kind of ice that only forms in thin sheets—sheets so thin that they would immediately break apart on contact—and, given its fragile, underdeveloped state, the *usurahi* was a sign that the harshest cold and most disagreeably severe period of winter had not yet come. The fact that we encounter *usurahi* in the brisk cold at the start of winter, I suppose, makes it even more beautiful.

The word itself has a nice ring to it, too. I wonder how it would sound if we were to call *usurahi* by some name like *hakuhyō* (thin ice), a term that is seen in the idiom *hakuhyō o fumu omoi da* (feeling as if one is treading on thin ice) and at ice rinks, where the areas of thin ice that ice skaters are prohibited from skating on are marked *hakuhyō kuiki* (thin-ice zones).

We would never, however, say "treading on thin ice" (*hakuhyō o fumu*) or "thin-ice zones" (*hakuhyō kuiki*) with the word *usurahi*: "treading on *usurahi*" or "*usurahi* zones." On the contrary, *usurahi* finds its best, most natural fit in expressions of "edges," in a way; when we feel a sense of awe at the sight of ancient remains or relish the emergence of the season when ice is still a rarity, *usurahi* is most appropriate.

I find the *ra* syllable sandwiched in the middle of *usarahi* particularly charming. *Usurahi* 薄氷 is thin (*usui*) ice (*hi*). Thin (*usui* 薄) can be shortened to *usu* 薄; *kōri* 氷 is also pronounced *hi* 氷; thus, you would expect this kind of ice to be called simply *usuhi*. But no—our forebears somehow managed to squeeze this *ra* in between these two words *usu* 薄 and *hi* 氷. The fact that *usuhi* never appears in the Japanese lexicon surely has something to do with the springy, light-hearted ring of that vestigial *ra* syllable.

Harusame

■ Spring Drizzle

*H*arusame is a shortened version of the phrase *haru no ame*, which literally means "spring rain," but the nuances of the two terms differ significantly. *Haru no ame* refers simply to the rain that falls during the temporal span of spring. *Harusame*, meanwhile, has its own distinctive resonance.

In Japan, rainy days are a common occurrence in the run-up to spring—the kind where your whole body gets enshrouded in a misty drizzle that grows ever softer and finer with each shower. In that light drizzle lies a certain charm; the term *en'u*, or fine misty drizzle, captures that aura with the Chinese characters "smoke" (*en* 煙) and "rain" (*u* 雨). After the drizzle reaches the *en'u* point, the rain enters the *harusame* realm.

When I was a university student, I attended a series of lectures by Kindaichi Haruhiko,[26] the late eminent professor of linguistics, titled "A Survey of Regional Dialects." In one lecture, Professor Kindaichi made the following remark: "*Harusame* falls only in Kyoto. It is rain that comes from below the ground. This rain is nothing like the stiff, hard rain that falls in Tokyo."

That remark—though I heard it more than fifty years ago—remains vivid in my memory today, a fact that testifies to the profound impression it made on me.

As someone born and raised in Tokyo, I was initially unable to understand what he meant. Decades later, however, during a week-long sojourn in Kyoto, I

26. Kindaichi Haruhiko (1913–2004)

はるさめ

suddenly understood. To my astonishment, it dawned on me that the *harusame* in Kyoto does indeed fall precisely in the way he had described: the rains really do seem to well up from below the ground. At that moment, I realized that rain that calls for an umbrella can never qualify as *harusame*.

It was also then that a certain line in a Shinkokugeki (New National Theater) comedy by playwright Yukitomo Kifū[27] called *Tsukigata Hanpeita* (1919), finally made sense. In that play, the protagonist Hanpeita finds himself caught in a shower as he leaves a certain establishment in the pleasure quarters accompanied by a young geisha. "It's raining!" (*Tsukisama, ame ga!*), the geisha exclaims, holding out her umbrella to him. "It's just a little *harusame*, darling," Hanpeita responds. "I'll just have to get a bit wet as we walk along!"

I doubt one would ever find a better explanation of *harusame* than this single line.

There is also a food in Chinese cuisine called *harusame*, a translucent noodle made mostly from some kind of potato. I have heard that it gets its name from its resemblance to *harusame* spring rains.

These *harusame* noodles are much thicker and fatter than *harusame* rain. The fact that the dish is named after *harusame*, though, betrays a uniquely elegant refinement.

27. Yukitomo Kifū (1877–1959)

Yūdachi

■ Sudden Evening Showers

Tere are several reasons why *yūdachi* rains have long been a Japanese favorite.

The term *yūdachi* refers to the big fat droplets of rain that fall on those hot summer days when you can't wait for evening to come, the kind of sudden rain that cools everything down. In one fell swoop, *yūdachi* takes care of all those annoying watering chores you still have to do: spraying the road, watering the plants. The energy of a *yūdachi* is hard to miss.

Yūdachi rains are sometimes accompanied by rolling thunder, giving them an even more summer-like feel.

I was told that a *yūdachi* forms way up high among the cumulonimbus clouds and then falls down through the cloud paths, which explains why the *yūdachi* rain lets up once the clouds have passed by.

Yes, I really am talking about those familiar clouds—the kind that billow up in thick bunches, high in the sky, painting the background of what a summer day looks like in the imagination. Who would ever think that those majestic clouds would produce *yūdachi* rain?

Sadly, with my poor knowledge of the natural sciences, I could never quite understand it.

But when I did finally learn that there is, in fact, a connection between cumu-

lonimbus clouds and *yūdachi*, I came to appreciate just what makes *yūdachi* rain such a magnificent kind of rain. You could probably just as well call *yūdachi* by a different name—*nyūdōame* (入道雨), or "cumulonimbus rain"—since it comes from the paths of thunderclouds, after all.

Yūdachi rain swoops down in one, forceful stroke. Suddenly hit by a *yūdachi* downpour, people frantically take cover under the eaves of buildings, or leap outside to bring in their laundry that's been hanging out to dry, or simply gaze up at the sky in astonishment.

Each of these scenes is a frame composing the image of all the *yūdachi* rains I have encountered in my life.

The rain itself comes down in great droplets that produce an even greater sound. The parched leaves of the trees and plants make a wet, crunching sound as the rain hits in heavy pellets, resounding with an especially powerful effect on large-leaved varieties like the sunflower.

Whenever I think about *yūdachi*, it's always summer in my mind—summer performing at its most robust, the rain a stout, nonchalant summer action.

When we recall memories of summer, thunderclouds and *yūdachi* rains are fixtures in the picture. That might very well be what nurtures our affection for the word.

Niwatazumi

Puddles of Rainwater

Niwatazumi is generally written with the Chinese character 潦. In antiquity, the word was written as *nihatazumi*. There are several theories about the word's origins, but it's impossible to say which is correct. Some say that *niwatazumi* comes from *niwakamizu*—a combination of *niwaka* (sudden) and *mizu* (water)—which suggests a pool of water that appears unexpectedly. Others say its correct reading is *niwatatsumizu*—a combination of *niwa* (garden), *tatsu* (to appear), and *mizu* (water)—which suggests a pool of water that forms in a garden.

In classical texts, the word denotes a puddle (*mizutamari*) that emerges as soon as rain has subsided. It usually appears as a descriptor of puddles that form here and there on the road.

We might expect that this phenomenon is seen often today. In our modern world, however, most roads and streets are paved, making it quite hard to find those types of puddles on the road; perhaps they now occupy the domain of nostalgia, the now-distant landscapes of our childhood.

That's why every time I hear the word *mizutamari*, fond memories of images and landscapes come to me.

The word *mizutamari* refers specifically to the small puddles of rainwater, of course. But in those tiny pools, I remember, were reflections of so many different things; even the distant sun appeared in those puddles, shining in a blinding flicker of light.

にわたずみ

Other times, the blue skies of autumn would appear in them, upside-down, with the clouds streaming along slowly in the water. I never seemed to tire of gazing at those inverted reflections of the heavens.

You might even say that puddles are repositories of the most precious memories from our youth.

However, the classical *niwatazumi* came to denote "sudden water" (*totsuzen no mizu*), thereby becoming a metaphor for the tears people shed on the occasion of someone's sudden death. That interpretation is obviously something altogether different from my romantic reminiscences.

The fearsome, violent connotations of this Chinese character for *niwatazumi*—潦—can be seen in the scene of Soga no Iruka's murder in the imperial court in 645. After being slashed to death in a veritable coup d'état, Iruka's corpse was tossed out into the rainy streets where, as the *Nihon Shoki* tells it: "Many puddles overflowed in the garden" (*niwatazumi, niwa ni iwameri*). The puddles formed in patches here and there around the corpse. Meanwhile, the rain did not let up: it grew only stronger, overflowing from the puddles and filling up the whole garden.

All those present, fearing implication in the murder, refused to approach the corpse. Hypocrites to the core, their undutiful, shallow hearts lay exposed for all to see—the *niwatazumi* overflowing into the garden. It was late summer, and the *samidare* (See page 90) rain continued to fall.

Shigure

■ Light Showers in Late Autumn and Early Winter

*S**higure* is the noun form of the verb *shiguru* (to drizzle), which is probably identical to the verb *shigurau*—a word that appears frequently in *Heike Monogatari* (*The Tale of Heike*, mid-thirteenth century).

It seems that *shigurau* was used to express the state of many things consolidating in a single place.

That's why, even today, rains in late autumn and early winter often go by the name *shigure* 時雨: the Chinese characters for "time" 時 (*toki*) and "rain" 雨 (*ame*). In short, these "occasional rains" (*toki no ame*, as some call them) fall all at once in a single, consolidated downpour at a certain time.

Moreover, *shigure* rains come just as the bitter winter cold starts to arrive. The rainy sky turns dark and water-laden. So long as these intermittent scattered showers—sometimes called *furimi furazumi*—refuse to let up, our hearts remain sulky and dejected.

Shigure is a forlorn, lonesome kind of rain. While that brooding pathos matches perfectly with the ever-present sadness in our hearts, there are times when it evokes a familiar intimacy. A poem by Paul Verlaine, which Horiguchi Daigaku famously translated into Japanese, begins with the following two lines:

"Il pleure dans mon coeur" (1874) "There is Weeping in My Heart"

Il pleure dans mon coeur There is weeping in my heart,
Comme il pleut sur la ville like the [*shigure*] rain falling on the town

In short, this is the type of rain that has become synonymous with the melancholy of the city.

Of course, Japanese *waka* poets have sung of the *shigure* rains for centuries, as far back as the *Man'yōshū*. One of my favorite poems is this poem:

Urasaburu	I am filled with loneliness
kokoro samaneshi	as I watch the flow of rain shower
hisakata no	falling from the sky,
ama no shigure no	from the long,
nagarafu mireba	long-continuing sky.

Osada no Ōkimi[28]

This excellent *tanka* appears in Book 1 of the *Man'yōshū*. The lonely *shigure* rains, as this poem suggests, produce a feeling of such tremendous sadness that you can feel the heavy gloom spreading throughout your whole body, eliciting thoughts of your own mortality.

The *shigure* rains have been known to inspire heartwarming compositions, as well. Take this modern haiku, for instance:

Shigururu ya	A shower in early winter—
eki ni nishiguchi	at this station a West Exit
higashiguchi	an East Exit.

Azumi Atsushi[29]

Years ago, when there was a sudden downpour of rain, crowds of people would congregate at train stations, waiting for their families to return from work or school. Here, too, the poet seems to meet someone at the station—but, alas, he isn't sure which exit they're at.

This familiar scene of someone waiting for a loved one to appear is a sweet one, indeed, and the *shigure* rains of bygone days surely provided the perfect stage for those warm feelings. Such scenes may very well occur today, too, of course, but people nowadays can use collapsible umbrellas, which are readily available. One can almost always find a taxi, too. The consequence of all that technological innovation, however, is that human connections have grown shallow. I feel nostalgia for that familiar *shigure* landscape, which is already a thing of the past.

28. Osada no Ōkimi (8th c.)   29. Azumi Atsushi (1907–1988)

Samidare
Early-Summer Rains

I am always surprised to find that so many people assume the word *samidare* —written "May" (五月) + "rain"(雨)— to be an etymological derivative of the word *satsukiame*—the rains (*ame*) of the fifth month (*satsuki*)—simply because the fifth month is called *satsuki*.

It is inconceivable, however, that the word *satsukiame* (fifth-month rains) could have somehow transformed into the word *samidare*. *Samidare* and *satsukiame* are completely different words altogether.

The word *samidare* appears in the *Kokin Wakashū* (ca. 905). When you look at the examples in that imperial anthology, *samidare* denotes a kind of violent rain that makes loud sounds as it falls, the kind of rain that throws you into a quiet, pensive mood. The fifth lunar month is the time of year when the "long rains" called *nagaame* fall in incessant, dreary sheets. The famous "love chats" (*ren'ai dangi*) in *Genji Monogatari* (*The Tale of Genji*, early eleventh century) also take place on those dreary nights, soaked with rain. Long ago, these rains no doubt produced unhygienic conditions that led to countless outbreaks of plagues and pestilence as well.

In short, what used to be called the *samidare* rains appear to have been the kind of rains that somehow "disturb"—*midareru* in Japanese—the human heart in one way or another. The fact that the first syllable of *samidare* is *sa* is likely proof that people regarded this disconcerting rain to be the work of a deity. Assuming this line of reasoning is true and *midare* is in fact the origin of the word *samidare*, I am deeply moved by the genius of the early modern Japanese for taking human emotions and naming a type of rain after them. Matsuo Bashō's famous haiku about *samidare* is clearer in that light, with the rains reflecting

sentiments of the heart.

> Samidare no　　Have the summer rains
> furinokoshite ya　come and gone, sparing
> hikari-dō　　　the Hall of Light?

Here, Bashō extols the exquisite beauty and venerable nobility of Konjikidō Golden Hall in Hiraizumi, Iwate Prefecture, which continuously preserved its radiant illumination without letting that sheen ever succumb to centuries of ominous rain. Bashō tuned his lyrical sensibilities to the confrontation between natural catastrophe and aesthetic beauty. The great poet Yosa Buson however, writing in the next century, changed the nuance of the *samidare* idea when he wrote his famous haiku on the subject:

> Samidare ya　　Early-summer rains!
> taiga o mae ni　facing the swollen river
> ie niken　　　two houses.

In Buson's poem, it is the cluster of traditional rural houses that are contending with the natural disasters. By shifting the setting from the sacred Hall of Light to the humble, traditional rural houses of the secular world, Buson took a shot at Bashō, who retained a certain lyricism reminiscent of the *waka* tradition. You can almost see the self-satisfied look on Buson's face at having one-upped his predecessor. In his poem, Buson shifted the focus of the *samidare* rain from its somber, depressing feel to its destructive power.

Nagori
Sorrows of Parting

The term *nagori* comes from two words: "wave" (*nami* 波) and "leftovers" (*nokori* 残り). The word thus initially referred to those small waves that remain on the shoreline after the larger wave has receded.

When the Japanese of old first grasped this phenomenon and created a word for it, they did not find anything particularly lyrical or moving about its meaning. Their interest began at what the waves brought and left: the brackish seaweed in the hollows and the tiny creatures washed up on the shore.

It was in pursuit of those leftovers that birds would fly down to the shore and people would gather on the beach.

From an early point, however, people came to regard that *nagori* as a beautiful beach scene.

Moreover, I believe the reason our forebears regarded this scene of people and birds gathering on the beach as beautiful was that their hearts were naturally inclined toward things that remain, and they regarded these accidental objects as gifts bestowed upon them from the legendary sea god called Watatsumi.

This is precisely why the association of the word *nagori* (the leftover wave) with actual ocean scenes quickly dissipated and took on primarily symbolic, metaphorical tones.

The word *nagori* eventually came to extend to all those remnant things that linger on in the aftermath of their sources, whether an actual thing or something less tangible, serving pragmatically as a linguistic expression signifying myriad things that fade incompletely—the *nagori* of such-and-such phenomena, as we say.

Take, for instance, the expression "leftover moon" (*nagori no tsuki*). This refers to the figure of the waning crescent moon in its last quarter, after passing the full-moon phase, and lingering whitely in the sky just as dawn starts to break.

Another is the term "leftover snow" (*nagori no yuki*), or snow that falls unexpectedly, despite winter having passed, seemingly unable to accept the fact that winter is over.

Nagori, it would appear, is used only in contexts involving a reluctance or unwillingness to part with something.

Now, if you'll recall the origin of the term—the little waves that remain on the shore after the main wave has receded—then you can see just how far the term *nagori* has traveled on its journey from its first meaning.

What all these *nagori* terms reveal is the extent to which humanity is unable or unwilling to let go of the past, to part with things that must inevitably pass away. And if you, like me, regard this essential facet of human feelings as something beautiful, the next time you close your eyes, you will no doubt see in your own heart too the image of a shoreline glistening after the wave has ebbed.

Nagori

なごり

Miotsukushi

Channel Markers

*M*iotsukushi refers to markers in the water indicating a shipping channel. The *miotsukushi* in Naniwa Bay, in fact, were the inspiration for the current emblem of Osaka City.

Under the ocean surface are countless coral rocks that are invisible to the naked eye from above the water. In the depths of the sea, meanwhile, there are also powerful undulations. These underwater elements make marine navigation difficult, much more than you might expect. I once inspected a nautical chart and was astonished to see the complexity of all the concavities and convexities and tidal current changes lurking down below.

This may seem like an odd association, but I once wondered how those markers at airports could control the landings and take-offs of so many airplanes on the runway strip—especially given the vast size of most airports. Then, I noticed a white line drawn on the ground for runway use. These white lines are essentially what we would call *miotsukushi: mio tsu kushi* 水脈つ串, which literally means the skewer (*kushi*) that indicates a water vein (*mio*). That's when I realized that an airport (*kūkō* 空港)—literally, "sky port" (*sora no minato*)—is also a harbor (*minato* 港) of sorts, just for airplanes rather than boats.

We call this navigation marker a *miotsukushi* because it means a skewer (*kushi*) that indicates the waterway channel (*mio*). While precise white lines can be drawn on airport runways, such exact lines cannot be drawn on the surface of the ocean. The "skewers" in the ocean hold the triangular signs marking the way.

When the word *mio*, signifying a sea lane, found its way into the classical canon, its meaning shifted, though. It came to connote *mi o tsukusu*, which means "to devote oneself entirely to something." Eventually, the new *mio* meaning replaced the old one altogether.

This play on *mi o tsukusu* and *miotsukushi* even appears in the famed classical anthology *Ogura Hyakunin Isshu*.[30] The term appears in two poems—Poems 20 and

---

30. *Ogura Hyakunin Isshu* (One Hundred Poems by Hundred Poets) complied by Fujiwara no Teika (1162–1241)

みおつくし

88—with the meaning of "to burn with love" (*koi ni mi o kogasu*).

The first of these two poems, Poem 20, is the following passionate *tanka* composed by Prince Motoyoshi:[31]

Wabinureba	Like a channel buoy
ima hata onaji	bobbing off Naniwa Bay
naniwa naru	my name is tossed about.
mi o tsukushite mo	But still I will come to you—
awamu to zo omou	though it be death to proceed[32]

The poem describes the time Prince Motoyoshi had an illicit love affair with Hōshi, the wife of Emperor Uda. Punning on the phrase "channel buoys in Naniwa Bay" (*Naniwa no miotsukushi*), it expresses Motoyoshi's "heart of burning love."

When you imagine Prince Motoyoshi's heart burning up with passion, you might envision that other world, one separate from that of sea and sky: the vast, uncharted space that has no roads or markers to guide us through.

The world I'm referring to is life itself.

Would that we each had some sort of *miotsukushi* to help us navigate our lives. No doubt we have all harbored that wish at one time or another. The author Tonomura Shigeru,[33] born and raised in the area around Lake Biwa, once wrote an autobiographical novel called *Miotsukushi* (1960), which won the Yomiuri Prize in 1960. In that novel, Tonomura's narrator transposes the *miotsukushi* from Lake Biwa onto his own life, using the channel markers to guide his readers through his story.

31. Prince Motoyoshi (890–943)   32. See note 3 on page 301   33. Tonomura Shigeru (1902–1961)

Uzumibi

■ Embers under Ash

L ong ago, people used to put charcoal (*sumi*) into a *hibachi* brazier to keep themselves warm. They would congregate in large numbers and surround large *hibachi* heaters, for example, or gather in small groups around a small *hibachi* to hold their hands in front of the fire. These days, however, tea furnaces —the kind used in *cha no yu* ceremonies—are the only places you can find *hibachi* charcoal still being used.

Here's how the charcoal was used. A person would take the remaining embers of the charcoal and then reuse them as the source for the next fire. The idea was to bury the smoldering embers under ash to keep the fire alive—so long as the embers continue to smolder beneath that layer of ash, the fire would mysteriously live on. When one would sift through the ashes, they would find a glow underneath, like a bright-red ruby revealing itself.

People used to call that hidden fire the *uzumibi*, or "buried flame." "Immersed flame" (*uzumatteiru hi*) might be another graceful expression for the same curious phenomenon. The term *uzumibi* refers to a flame that burns forth continuously yet inconspicuously, creating a beautiful radiance at once exquisite and invisible. This exquisite flame is a far cry from some piteous fire completely buried, long forgotten.

When I was a boy, we used to have a verb for expressing this act of applying ash onto the coal: *ikeru*. I can recall how my mother used to say, "Be sure to *ikeru*

the ashes before you go to sleep, son."

So, what exactly does this transitive verb *ikeru* mean, though? Today, the verb has gone out of use, relegated to the category of "dead words," or *shigo*. Yet it does survive as a component of several other terms. Take *ikegaki*, for instance— literally, a "fence that lets the surrounding plants and shrubbery live"—which refers to a hedge of trees, bamboo, or other living plants in a trimmed row, forming a fence. Another term is *ikesu*—literally, a "holding pool (*su*) that lets the fish live"—a tank that keeps fish alive. These two terms suggest the notion of something allowing a natural phenomenon to occur or be as is: *ikashite oku*, as we say in our contemporary idiom. Letting the trees live as they are. Letting the fishes be. Letting things thrive as they are.

In short, the act of putting ash on the charcoal to preserve the fire underneath was called *hai o ikeru*, literally to keep the fire alive. Without someone present to scoop more ash onto the charcoal, the charcoal would burn out and die. By continuously tossing ash onto the smoldering flame and creating a so-called *uzumibi*, however, one could preserve the life of the charcoal for as long as they like.

This term *uzumibi*, or "buried flame," thus denotes a flame whose life force is animated and sustained.

The poignant notion of *uzumibi* offers a rich metaphor for our human lives.

Uzumibi

うずみび

Kitsunebi

Will-o'-the-Wisp

The fox—*kitsune* in Japanese—is perhaps the most well-loved animal in Japan, with the possible exception of one or two other species.

A bowl of *soba* buckwheat noodles is called *kitsunesoba* just because it has a single piece of deep-fried tofu on top. The *nagareya*, or stray arrow that shoots off into the air without striking any object, is called *kitsuneya*—literally a "fox arrow." No doubt the fox finds these uses of its name rather annoying.

Among the other terms that use the word *kitsune*—no doubt to the fox's disliking—is *kitsunebi*, literally "fox fire," which refers to the visual phenomenon where mysterious lights appear at night. According to folklorists, the term comes from the rather implausible legend that foxes possess the ability to spew fire from their mouths. Moreover, in haiku, *kitsunebi* is a seasonal word (*kigo*) for winter, suggesting that the legends about it were taken to be true.

The roots of that mysterious "fox fire" lie in an imagined resemblance to the intense fire that results from burning phosphorus. Long ago, it was customary for people to say that cemeteries would sometimes shine with the light of ignis fatuus—dead spirits in the forms of floating ghost lights, or *hitodama* 人魂 in Japanese—that glow in blue hues, which they apparently attributed to phosphorus burning inside the bones of buried corpses. Legend has it that foxes would gnaw on the bones for sustenance, and the phosphorus from the bones would begin to burn—and that led to the foxes spewing the fire from their mouths.

When the story has reached this point, it is no longer clear whether it was the foxes playing tricks on humans or the humans deceiving the foxes. The humans could have very well been blaming foxes all this time for their own lies and nefarious activities.

There are various other ways to express the *kitsunebi* phenomenon. One way is the phrase "fox's lanterns" (*kitsune no chōchin*), which gets its name from the image of lanterns hanging in a sequential pattern.

This series of lights has also been likened to a wedding procession. With that logic, you might think the phrase *kitsune no yomeiri*—literally, "fox's wedding"—would be a line of "fox fires" (*kitsunebi*).

However, the phrase refers to the phenomenon of *hideri-ame* (sun shower), or a spot of passing rain on a sunny day, which is inconsistent with the "fox fires" (*kitsunebi*) of those mystifying nighttime lights. On second thought, maybe the phrase suggests that the fox, on a moonlit night, causes it to rain? Could it be that foxes emit fire from their mouths in the rain and set off a "wedding procession" of light in place of lanterns? If that fanciful story is true, it's certainly a rather elaborate contrivance.

I think that we humans love using foxes as material for coming up with the wild, fanciful stories we tell ourselves.

Winter is when talk of *kitsunebi* comes up most often. The combination of the *kitsunebi*'s rather spooky, ethereal overtones and winter's brooding mood makes all those dubious stories even more spine-chilling. Even the great haiku poet Yosa Buson exploited those associations in verse, composing the following poem:

> Kitsunebi ya   Fox fire!
> dokuro ni ame no   On a night when the skull
> tamaru yoru ni   gathers rain
> > Yosa Buson

You can see just how enchanting the fanciful *kitsunebi* phrase must have been for the people of old—look at how many fantasies and images it inspired. Surely, I can't be the only one with the urge to scribble out a poem on that magical subject!

Words about the Four Seasons and Living Things

Haru

■ Spring

When you live abroad for some time, you realize that Japan is one of the few countries in the world with four distinct seasons that unfold at just the right differences in temperature.

Japan's natural climate exhibits seasonal changes that are not possible with most regions. Even some countries with four seasons experience little variation in temperature. Some people find it difficult to live in Japan's climatic flux: one is constantly having to adjust their clothes to the season, their air conditioning to the changing temperatures, and so forth. Those complaints might ring true from a purely utilitarian standpoint. To my mind, however, Japan's drastic seasonal changes are invaluable and instrumental in making the country splendidly *seasonable.*

The first season of the year is spring: *haru* 春. Chinese characters with the same phonetics in Japanese—*haru*—abound: 張る (*haru*), 晴る (*haru*), and 墾 る (*haru*), to name a few. They all connote a similar nuance: something agreeable, something natural and unstrained, something of a carefree disposition. Spring, then, is the season when greenery flourishes, when the heart is free to swell with joy—the season of *haru* (張る). Spring is also the season when the clouds that have blocked the sky through the long winter finally depart: the season of *haru* (晴る). It is also the season when the cropped winter fields are cleared and reclaimed for cultivation, the season of *haru* (墾る). In short, spring—the season when all of these *haru* things occur—was, fittingly, *haru* in the classical Japanese mind.

Today, in Japan, people only distinguish between summer clothes and winter clothes. So when people use the term *koromogae* 衣更—which means the seasonal change of clothes—they generally mean the wardrobe changes that happen at the start of winter and the start of summer. Long ago, however, people used another word: *harugoromo* 春衣 (spring clothing). Taking off their heavy winter clothing and donning lighter spring attire—that is, by changing into *harugoromo*—people perceived the coming of spring on a sensory level. Do you not detect the remnant trace of this dead word *harugoromo* in the phrase "taking off one's gloves?" In my view, *harugoromo* is a term that people should start using again.

When *haru* comes to Japan, you find that the fields and mountains suddenly brighten with a profusion of flowers. Given the sizable disparities in latitude among the various regions of Japan, this explosion of growth comes at different times. *Haru*, though, is the season when most places experience a continuous blossoming, a dizzying spectacle that progresses in a predetermined sequence: daphne flowers (*jinchōge*), camellia (*tsubaki*), plum blossoms (*ume*), cherry blossoms (*sakura*), peach blossoms (*momo*), and finally kerria (*yamabuki*). When the wisteria (*fuji*) start to bloom, you know that spring has passed into summer. The shrubbery, too, proclaims the arrival of spring: Thunberg spiraea (*yukiyanagi*), forsythia (*rengyō*), and Scotch broom (*enishida*) appear to herald spring's arrival.

Enveloped in these myriad images and associations, *haru* is a word that floats up to our ears with a scintillating, lighthearted sound; the brightness of the word is unmistakable.

Haru is the season when our hearts flutter with excitement. In fact, a medical scholar once told me that human beings secrete a special hormone during the spring months. The word has such an immense presence, I think, because it embodies such a rich assortment of associations.

Haru

はる

Urara
■ Bright, Beautiful Spring Weather

U *rara* expresses the easy-going, laid-back feel of spring weather. This mood is conveyed in the popular song: *Haru no urara no Sumidagawa!* "Bright, beautiful spring has come over the Sumida River!" In Chinese characters, the most common rendering of *urara* is the character *rei* 麗, which means "beautiful" or "bright." We also sometimes find *urara* written with the character 遅 (late, slow, or gentle), as in the well-known expression *shunjitsu uraura* 春日遅々, which means a slow-moving, serene spring day.

Yet if you consider the meaning of *urara* as a native Japanese word, rather than in terms of Chinese characters, you find that neither 麗 (beautiful) nor 遅 (gentle) are entirely appropriate.

Urara is the shortened form of *ura-ura*. This means that the *ura* component forms the word's core. If you gather up all the closely related terms, however, you find among them various moisture-related expressions that begin with *uru* (the root form of *ura*), such as "wet with moisture" (*uruoi ga aru*) and "eyes wet with tears" (*me mo urumu*). It is also common in conversational speech to hear someone say they are so sad that "even their heart is wet with tears" (*kokoro mo uruuru*). It follows, then, that we can only call something *urara* when it has an abundance of moisture permeating it. I suppose that's why we most often hear the word *urara* in spring, the time of year when the air is full of moisture.

At the same time, we also use *urara* in the autumn (*aki*)—"*aki urara*," as we say, which means "a clear autumn air"—to capture the still, brisk autumn air that reminds us of a spring day. In short, *urara* can be used to express a moist, bright day in spring, but it can also be used to convey a calm, peaceful day in autumn.

The famous line from the *Kojiki*, attributed to Yamato Takeru no Mikoto—"How beautiful is Yamato!" (*Yamato shi uruwashi*)—is another expression that clearly evokes the natural climate of the Yamato region when it is gently shrouded in that unmistakable soft spring haze.

Even though today we may use the Chinese character *rei* 麗 (bright, beautiful) for the native Japanese word *uruwashii*, I'd still like it to be a word that evokes a beauty that is overflowing with such gentle feelings and associations.

It follows, then, that a person who is regarded as a *reijin* 麗人 or "beautiful person" is not simply someone with well-defined facial features. Rather, a true *reijin* must also possess a certain moisture, a kind of supple freshness that complements their outward beauty.

Similarly, the word *utsukushii* (beautiful) did not originally denote physical beauty alone. It also connoted a sweet-natured, adorable, and lovely nature. Like *reijin*, *utsukushii* requires a certain gentleness of manner in addition to the element of physical beauty. Clearly, Japanese conceptions of beauty have always been linked to human sentiment and matters of the heart.

Urara

うらら

Natsu

■ Summer

Japanese people have grown so accustomed to the four seasons (*shiki* 四季) that we are invariably shocked when we hear that many ancient civilizations—ancient Greece, for instance—had only three seasons. Still, there was a certain logic to having only three seasons.

Humans originally divided the year into two seasons: the warm season, when they could work in the open outdoors, and the cold season, when they had to work inside. The latter was "winter" (*fuyu*). The "outdoor-work" season eventually split into two seasons—spring and autumn, as the well-known Chinese phrase 春耕秋収 suggests: "planting in spring" (春耕) and "harvesting in autumn" (秋収). The premodern Japanese divided the year into three seasons: spring and autumn (the two seasons of outdoor work) and then winter. Thus, we can see that summer was the last season to come into being.

The custom of sowing, cultivating, and harvesting has served as the bedrock of sustaining human life and civilization. In relatively stable climates with minimal temperature variation, people divide the seasons according to human activity: plowing the soil in spring and reaping the harvest in autumn. In those conditions, it is only natural that there should be just three seasons.

But when you add in the "hot" summer as its own independent season, you get the familiar four-season arrangement. A certain aesthetic precision—a certain sensitivity that transcends the simple, functional dynamic of "work"—comes into play, making the year all the more wonderful.

The word *natsu*, then, is most likely derived from the property of heat, called *atsu* 暑 in Japanese. Spring is moderate, pleasantly warm. Autumn is brisk and cool. Squeezed between these two seasons is the newly added season of "hot summer" (*atsui natsu*), the season when the crops ripen. You can almost feel the love and anticipation that our ancestors felt as they watched the fruits of the fields slowly ripening in the summer heat. Simply sowing the seeds never yielded a harvest, now, did it? Our forebears gave that ripening stage a name distinct from the spring and fall.

Summer began in this way, and so it is the season when humans, too, must mature and ripen in the sweltering heat. Under the bright glare of the blazing sun, we do not put aside our studies but instead apply our efforts ever more diligently in our pursuit of knowledge. The fact that even today we engage in summer-camp schools and summer courses is not a demonstration of our willingness to study during the midsummer break. Rather, it is a testament to our desire to learn *in* the hot summer itself. In Buddhism, there is even a type of rigorous spiritual training called *geango* 夏安居, which is a three-month summer retreat during which people confine themselves and practice an ascetic way of life. The term originally meant "confining oneself inside in the rainy season" (*amagomori*).

The cool of the evening, the wind chimes tinkling, the shaved ice—all the signature symbols of soothing relief from the summer heat coalesce into distinctive features of the Japanese summer—but they never try to resist or contend with the summer heat. Rather, they represent a harmonious attempt to coexist with the heat, to produce a cooling state within that very heat.

As such, we can say that the summer matures us humans, ripening us into full-fledged beings. For centuries, Japanese people have cherished the word *natsu*—a term expressing the fiery passion to grow and develop despite the intense heat.

Natsu
———
なつ

Tokonatsu

Eternal Summer

Tokonatsu means "eternal summer." *Toko* is rendered with the Chinese character 常, normally pronounced *tsune*—which means that one might easily conflate the *toko* nuance with the connotations of *tsune*, or something usual and customary. However, the two are quite different.

Take two examples of words with the *toko* variant: *tokoshie* (forever) and *tokoyo* (eternal world). *Toko*, then, evokes the idea of limitless, infinite time.

Incidentally, *toko* and its close relative *toki* both refer to time. Where the distinction between the two lies is in their scale: the former signifies time as an abstract concept, while the latter denotes the reality of time in a limited, determinative sense.

Then there is the seasonal flower that often goes by the nickname "eternal summer" (*eien no natsu*). The flower's actual name is *nadeshiko*, or the "fringed pink" (dianthus superbus) in English.

Did you know that the charming little *nadeshiko* flower blooms in midsummer with such rich vitality? In the old lunar calendar, summer spans from the fourth month to the sixth month. In a solar calendar, the summer solstice is in the sixth month and the autumnal equinox is in the ninth month.

After I learned of these different timing conventions, I decided to track the blooming patterns of the *nadeshiko* flower for a few years. I then discovered that, indeed, the flower appears as early as the fourth month in the solar calendar and lingers around until as late as the tenth month. True to its nickname, the "eternal summer," the *nadeshiko* flower blooms for an impressive duration. The blossoms last so long that the *nadeshiko* is even one of the "seven wild flowers of autumn" (*aki no nanakusa*).

The Koreans used the resilient plants' roots and seeds for medicinal purposes, so they must have been aware of the fact that *nadeshiko* were not just pretty plants but also filled with nutritious value.

Naturally, the flowering period's peak comes in the sixth month of the old lunar calendar. That month also goes by another name: the *tokonatsuzuki*, or, fittingly, the "month of the eternal summer."

Considering its lengthy blooming period and tendency to flower at the height of summer, the *nadeshiko* is quite the resilient flower.

Long ago, Japanese people referred to the women of their country as *Yamato nadeshiko*, a term that signifies the epitome of pure feminine beauty. The Chinese characters for *nadeshiko*—撫子—equate to "caressable child." After the Second World War, however, this designation for women was highly criticised. It met with opposition because it seemed to ascribe a kind of slavish obedience and weakness to women. I suppose that impression of servility comes mostly from the connotations of the term's written rendering (caressable child) and the implications of the word *naderu* 撫でる (caress) itself.

But when you consider the fact that *nadeshiko*'s alternative name is *tokonatsu*, learn more about the plant's botany, and understand the actual nature of the flower's blooming, you come to see that *nadeshiko* is a strong species with an exquisitely beautiful flower. I personally see no need to avoid comparing women to the *nadeshiko*.

Why not call this flower by its other name—*tokonatsu*?

Tokonatsu

とこなつ

Aki

◼ Autumn

It seems that the word *aki* (autumn) has close connections to *aki* 飽き, whose original meaning connotes full satisfaction. No doubt some will claim that these two words clearly had different phonological origins. The difference, however, is not one of phonology but rather a change in pronunciation. Even if we acknowledge that distinction, the two words are still close companions.

Needless to say, there has always been a close connection between the autumn season and the bountiful, sating harvest. For humans, autumn is by far the most crucial season of the year.

There are several Chinese characters for the concept of *year*. One is 載 (*noru/ sai*: to load into a cart), which suggests harvest fertility, or *minori* 稔り in Japanese. The annual year is also expressed with the character *sai* 歳, as in the expression *senzai ichigū*, meaning "one chance in a thousand years." This custom of expressing the year (normally 年) with the alternative character *sai* 載 (to load into a cart) reflects the fact that, once a year, people would load the harvest yield into their carts.

During the bountiful autumn harvest, an array of colors floods the fields and mountains. Europeans probably envision bunches of grapes dangling from trees when they think of autumn. In Japan, however, it is the persimmon, or *kaki*, that has long reigned as the "king of the fruits"; Japanese people will no doubt associate autumn with its branches.

In autumn, our mountains, too, take on the hues of bright crimson and yellow as the trees change color and nature's rich colors spread out before one's eyes.

Since antiquity, Japanese people have preserved the custom of holding annual autumn festivals to give thanks to Shinto deities. They offer the first fruits of the autumn harvest to the deities as tokens of gratitude.

Deep down, we all desire to experience such a glorious harvest in whatever way we can: how smart we've grown through reading, how many work goals we have accomplished, and how our health is improving. So much comes back to that idea of reaping and sowing.

Some time ago, the neologism *shishūki* 思秋期—derived from the actual word *shishunki* 思春期, which means puberty—came into vogue. Playing on puberty (*shishunki*) by replacing *shun* 春 (spring, also pronounced *haru*) with *shū* 秋 (autumn, or *aki*), the word refers to a mature romance that one might experience late in life—the "spring" of youth in one's "autumn" years. As the popularity of this word suggests, autumn is certainly not the year's loneliest season.

When the cold *shigure* rains start to fall, the autumn scene transforms into a lonesome landscape. But this transformation, remember, is just the *shigure* rains turning autumn to winter.

If anything, autumn is a bright, joyous time.

Simply uttering the word *aki* makes us feel as though we're soaring up high up in the clear autumn skies, satisfied as can be.

Aki
——
あき

Koharu-biyori

■ Balmy Autumn Days

*K*oharu-biyori contains the word *haru,* meaning spring. However, the term denotes the "splendid weather" (*hiyori*) that suddenly emerges in the middle of the tenth month.

By "tenth month," of course, I don't mean October in the Gregorian calendar. Rather, I mean the tenth month of the old lunar calendar. After we've shifted everything over a month, the tenth month corresponds to November in the modern calendar—which is even colder. And yet somehow, out of this brisk cold, an almost spring-like, splendid day (*hiyori*) appears out of the blue. Since antiquity, Japanese people have expressed their delight at this brief respite from the cold.

You might find my interpretation rather ingenious, I suppose, but the truth is that I couldn't understand this expression *koharu-biyori* for the life of me when I was a kid. I'd flip through my Japanese-English dictionaries in search of an explanation, but all I'd find were a few remarks about how the word corresponds to the English phrase "Indian summer." *What on earth is that supposed to mean?* I'd wonder with a sigh.

The almost gallingly strange and sublime qualities of the Japanese language crystallize in the workings of this single word *koharu-biyori.* Take the first syllable, *ko* 小, which is the Japanese word for "small." How is it conceivable that a season—spring, in this case—could be described as "small?" Despite that logical confusion, the Japanese language has long affixed this *ko* diminutive prefix or suffix to all manner of nouns, at times even inserting it to suggest faint (or small) impressions. We see this, for example, in the word *o-kogoto,* which means "fault-finding." Take *ko-nikurashii,* an adjective meaning "slightly irritating or annoying." We even see it at times in people's names: the great female poet of the Heian period, Ono no Komachi,[1] for instance, whose name combines "small" (*ko* 小) + "town" (*machi* 町) to signify "girl."

---

1. Ono no Komachi (ca. 825–ca. 900)

こはるびより

Then there's *koharu*, which uses the term *haru* (spring) to express a phenomenon that occurs in winter. Japanese people have never felt any qualms about separating the natural seasons into two distinct phenomena: the seasons themselves and the human perceptions thereof. Indeed, we even regard subjective perceptions of a season as more important than the actual season itself: the late-autumn seasonal word "winter-like midnight cold" called *yosamu* makes you believe it to be winter until you remember that it's still autumn outside. Likewise, we devised expressions for spring without using the word *haru* (spring): to evoke the image of spring haze (*harugasumi*), one can simply say *kasumi* (haze). Or to convey autumn fog (*akigiri*), all one needs is the word *kiri* (fog). The prominence of such seasonal words (*kigo*) reflects the extent to which Japanese people have always lived according to our inner sensibilities and sensory impressions rather than objective observations of the natural world.

Then there's this matter of the word *hiyori* 日和, which refers to the general state of the weather. The term was originally written with the Chinese characters *hi* 日 (day) and *yori* 寄り (drawing together), which is more fitting than the current way of writing it with 日 (day) + 和 (harmony). By describing the weather (*higara*)—that is, the "personality" (*gara*) of the day (*hi*)—in terms of favorable or lucky or good (*kyō wa o-higara mo yoi*) as is often said, our ancestors went so far as to ascribe human-like personality to the day. Even the sudden changes in weather throughout the day were attributed to the day's moods swings.

All of these qualities—the use of the diminutive prefix *ko*, the subjectification of the seasons, the anthropomorphization of the daily weather—converge in this single word *koharu-biyori*, which kindles a quiet, subdued pleasure. Long ago, it was on *koharu-biyori* days that fathers would bundle their families up in scarves and take them on a stroll to pay their respects at the nearby Shinto shrine. With the full knowledge that this would be their last warm day for a while, in their hearts they sheltered hopes for the coming spring.

Fuyu
Winter

*F*uyu 冬 is probably the same word as the archaic word *hiyu* 冷ゆ, from which the modern verb *hieru* (to become cold) descends. *Fuyu* is the season when penetrating cold chills us to the bone; coldness is its most salient characteristic.

But why, exactly, did the premodern Japanese name the sensation of becoming cold *hiyu*?

In winter, people's bodies rattle and shake in the cold. In all contexts, Japanese people have long referred to this type of movement with the verb *furu* 振る. The two Chinese characters for earthquake—*jishin* 地震—used to be read *nai-furu*, for instance, connoting the idea that the earth shakes and shivers. Likewise, the word for a clock pendulum—an object that sways back and forth—is *furiko* 振子. The movement of bodies quavering, too, is called *furu*. Natural shaking is *fuyu* 振ゆ.

Fuyu 振ゆ (shaking and trembling) is doubtless the same word as the word *fuyu* 冬, winter. Thus, by simply changing *fu* to *hi*, they likely came up with verb *hiyu*, which expresses a chilling of the body.

Fuyu is shrouded in negative associations. Temperatures drop. Cold rains fall, leaving people soaking wet and prone to sickness. The landscape darkens. Daylight hours shorten. There seems to be nothing good whatsoever about the season.

However, these essential attributes are precisely what make winter what it is. The season cannot but have these qualities.

The word *fuyugomori*, meaning "winter confinement," captures the isolated, confined (*komori*) nature of winter (*fuyu*) itself. But the word also suggests the fact that humans, too, hide themselves indoors during the cold of winter—the word itself invokes both the nature of the season and the idea of "human hibernation."

Thus, it follows that winter is the season when our hearts turn inward. The repose of the cold months gives us the opportunity to realize things that we had completely forgotten about, owing to our usual busy distractions and the pressure of business matters.

We are more inclined, for example, to read books in winter. During the cold winter months, our greatest friends are the *kotatsu* (traditional heating table) and the *danro* (fireplace). Only in winter do we get the urge to read a book through the long night. Or to take out our brush and inkstone and practice our calligraphy. Or to write a long letter to a friend.

These winter customs might lead us to think that the word *fuyu* possesses a heavy, ponderous feel. However, the word also conveys a sedate dignity, one befitting an almost regal presence. We can take comfort in the stability of *fuyu*, like a trustworthy leader or a reliable friend.

Fuyu

ふゆ

Kisaragi
■ Second Month in the Old Lunar Calendar

Most Japanese people know that *kisaragi* denotes the second month in the old lunar calendar. The word probably comes from the phrase *ki sara ni ki*, which means something like "to put on the usual layers of clothing (*ki*) and then bundle up even further (*sara ni ki*)." This much is easy enough to understand.

From there, people lazily assume the word to be something all too obvious that warrants no further consideration. A closer look at the word's origin, however, reveals that it does have quite a distinctive feel.

In the modern calendar, the winter solstice—the shortest day of the year—comes in late December. In terms of the actual amount of solar heat that reaches Earth, one would think the winter solstice would be the coldest day of the year. But in fact, the thermometer continues to drop for another two full months, reaching its lowest temperature at last in February. Our forebears were right, then, to dub the extremely cold month of February *kisaragi*: *ki sara ni ki* (wearing layers upon layers of clothing).

The sight of people bundled up in layers of clothing is a humorous, amusing one. It seems that February is the time of year when we humans get along best with our fellows. Surely there is something about our dressing up like butterballs that softens the human heart.

Long ago, kimono were highly venerated because they were thought to carry within them the "spirits" of their owners. This explains why it was such a great honor to receive an article of clothing from the emperor—the recipient got a piece of the emperor's spirit with it, our forebears believed. These remnant living spirits were also thought to be present in passed-down kimonos, or *o-sagari*, which I will discuss on page 272. An *o-sagari* kimono from a sibling thus held a part of your brother or sister, wrapping itself around your body and protecting you from danger.

If you imagine a person bundled up in five or six layers of clothing, you can get a sense of just how well protected they are by the multiple souls lodging in their clothes: a total full-out assault from each article of clothing.

Indeed, since *kisaragi* involves layering various articles of clothing (and souls) into a warm sheath, one must make sure to receive these blessings while letting out a scream. For this is why dressing in layered clothing keeps us so warm— because of the souls inside.

Karotōsen
■ Useless Things

The expression *karotōsen* consists of four Chinese characters: 夏 summer + 炉 furnace + 冬 winter + 扇 folding fan.

The expression first appeared in ancient China, almost two millennia ago, in a book called the *Lunheng* (80 CE). When this book found its way to Japan, it gained a favorable response, and went on to offer an important new paradigm for reading literature.

The meaning of the phrase is plain: a hot-furnace (*ro*) in summer (*ka*) and a cooling fan (*sen*) in winter (*tō*). Accordingly, it refers to anything out of step with the season. The heat furnace (*ro*) equates to the fireplace in Europe and the traditional *irori* (a sunken hearth) in Japan. The term *ro* probably refers to the heater and heating appliances in today's idiom.

Heaters are indispensable in the winter, but they are completely useless in the summer. *Irori* in classic Japanese rooms sometimes get covered with a tatami mat during the summer months.

That's why the *karotōsen* served as a metaphor for anything that is completely useless.

But it was the great haikai poet Matsuo Bashō who suddenly made the expression famous in Japan. When asked what purpose his haikai poetry served, he famously replied in his "Kyoriku Ribetsu no Kotoba" (On Parting from Kyoriku, 1693), "The elegance of my poems is like a *karotōsen*." Bashō attracted a great number of people at the time with his new style of composition. Turning to his disciples, he told them that his haiku possessed absolutely no practical, utilitarian purpose. That rather brazen statement delivered a sizable shock to his followers and, eventually, the entire literary world.

What exactly did Bashō mean by his response? There is a famous Daoist phrase that might provide a hint: "The useless-looking thing is actually sometimes useful" (*muyō no yō*). I think that's what Bashō was aiming for in writing haiku.

It is a common phenomenon that things we deem useless unexpectedly play a major role in shaping things when left alone. Conversely, those devious, nitpicky types found in every company office are no more than petty functionaries who are of no real use to anyone. In haiku, too, we see the same thing in those superficial poets who fastidiously adhere to the rules of *kigo* (season words) without thinking deeply about the true impressions of each season (*kisetsukan*).

This term *karotōsen*, though, suggests a much grander perspective than the narrow worldview inhabited by petty flatterers and haiku poetasters who think only in terms of seasonal words. And those who are preoccupied with the prospects of immediate gain—the matter of whether a near-term thing is useful or useless—will never accomplish anything meaningful either, so long as they avoid engaging in self-fortifying experiences. Even today, we can hear the voices in our heads—whispers from time past—that remind us to put aside our petty concerns and value the basic way of life.

Karotōsen is certainly one word that I would like to continue to savor until my dying breath.

Yuki-onna
Snow Woman

The world of haikai poetry is a world of fantasy. It includes all kinds of fanciful creatures, *yōkai* spirits, and strange elements. Poets would describe, for instance, weeping turtles (*kame ga naku*). They would sing about *kamaitachi*—literally, "sickle weasels"—mythological animals that appear riding on dust devils, slicing into people with their sickle-like limbs.

In the real world, of course, no one has ever heard the actual cry of a turtle. And the word *kamaitachi*, in poetry, refers not to horrifying beasts but rather to the wind that "cuts" people as it passes by. The fact that haikai poets referred to the wind by the name *kamaitachi* suggests the fantastical vision of a weasel (*itachi*) wielding a sickle (*kama*).

The haikai literary form was the product of a humorous, bawdy response to the excessive seriousness and refinement of traditional Japanese *waka* poetry. To be sure, traditional *waka* poetry sometimes allowed for some degree of comical or fanciful daydreaming, so long as it was from the heart and referenced long-lost, faraway lovers. But *waka* poetry did not permit the inclusion of mysterious, fanciful images like crying turtles. Such flights of pure fancy were inelegant, low-brow from the *waka* perspective.

That is precisely why *waka*'s opposite—haikai—is so much fun. The unorthodox, brazen sensibility that produced the image of a female *obake* ghost emerging on a snowy evening is enough to send a gust of inspiring wind under the wings of our hearts.

Yuki-onna—literally, "snow woman"—refers to the legendary beauties of Japanese folklore who emerge from the woods on snowy nights. These alluring appa-

ゆきおんな

ritions were also called *yuki-jorō*—"snow harlots"—on account of their coquettish nature and sensual charms. They even went by the dazzling if not eerie name *yuki-oni*, or "snow demon." Yet another moniker, *yuki-bōzu*, or "snow rascals," had a more boyish nuance to it. Legends about these mystical "snow women" abound in folktales from all over Japan. Of the myriad existing legends, however, it was a *yuki-onna* from the northern prefecture of Iwate that renowned ethnologist and folklorist Yanagita Kunio[2] singled out as the subject for analysis in his classic study *Tōno Monogatari* (The Tales of Tōno, 1910). According to his description, the snow women of the Tōno region were believed to bring lost children home on the fifteenth night of the first lunar month known as "little New Year" (*koshōgatsu*), and on nights of the winter full moon.

The legends may be no more than sad fantasies spun by grieving mothers who had lost their own infants. According to another folk legend, people believed that it was in fact the great Buddhist monk and founder of the Shingon sect Kūkai[3] who escorted lost children back to their families. I suppose this is an example of what religion scholars call syncretism: the blending of multiple narratives from disparate traditions.

The lost children, escorted home by either *yuki-onna* or Kūkai in these legends, are probably themselves miniature "snow rascals" (*yuki-bōzu*).

In recent years, Japan's annual snowfall figures have dropped drastically. It often seems to me that the spiritual richness of the Japanese people has also grown impoverished in equal measure. Might there be a connection between the amount of snowfall and our depth of spirit?

2. Yanagita Kunio (1875–1962) 3. Kūkai (774–835)

Shitamoe
▪ Shooting Sprout

In early spring, the plant buds known as *shitamoe* shoot up from the soil in the mountains and fields. The promise of spring becomes manifest, visible. The grasses start to shoot forth. The sprouting of young buds, or *shitamoe* (a combination of the Chinese characters *shita* 下, for under or underneath, and *moe* 萌え, or a young bud sprouting into a leaf), begins.

I like how this word *shita* (underneath) is used in *shitamoe*. The term begins with *shita* because the process occurs under the surface, hidden from the naked eye, as the plant furtively starts to shoot its bud. A small bud appearing unimpeded above the flat surface of the earth, even in the smallest emergence, is not what we would call *shitamoe*.

It may appear to be little more than a rumbling under dried-up grass and winter trees in hues of dark gray, but *shitamoe* is just that—a budding from a hidden source, emerging from underneath.

The innate sense of emergence pervading *shitamoe* lends the word a nuance of discovery: the arrival of spring. Just as you think to yourself that spring is sadly still a long way away, you suddenly notice this little young bud and realize that spring has, in fact, already arrived. *Shitamoe* is a spark that causes hearts to dance and flutter with excitement.

The particularly inspiring dimension of *shitamoe* buds is how their discovery is a seasonal discovery that people hope for; we all have a natural inclination to celebrate spring as the season of joy and mirth. Spring is the time when people discover the great rebirth of Mother Earth, which had appeared to have all but

died out during the winter—our joy at that rejuvenation forever new.

I should say a word about the verb *moeru* (萌える), as well. The term, which means "to sprout" or "bud," suggests the process by which spring arrives. The premodern Japanese did not make any distinctions between the process of *moeru* 萌える—plants coming into life—and the process of *moeru* 燃える—fire burning.

Today, however, Japanese people tend to read the world through the lens of Chinese characters. Fire burns (*moeru* 燃える), as the Chinese character 燃 conveys. Plants grow (*moeru* 萌える), as the character 萌 suggests. People today assume that these two terms' identical pronunciations are a mere coincidence, but the fact of the matter is that the words themselves precede their Chinese scripts. Originally, Japanese people would use *moeru* 燃える (to burn) and *moeru* 萌える (to grow) in the same sense, with both referring to the same phenomenon; in other words, the distinction between the two developed only after the distinction in the Chinese characters took hold.

Trees and vegetation are constantly *burning (moeru* 燃える) life itself, *inochi* 命, in a combustive process—one example of the cycle of regeneration and rebirth.

In the discovery of life's waking moments, those first clear stirrings of spring, lies an inimitable spark of joy—the emotion that inspired the word *shitamoe* in the first place.

Tsuratsura Tsubaki

■ Japanese Camellia

henever someone mentions the *tsubaki* (camellia tree), I immediately think of that slippery-smooth oil for cooking and dressing hair called *tsubaki abura* (camellia oil). When I imagine *tsubaki* flowers blooming, however, I can never fully reconcile the two images of oil and blossoms, no matter how hard I try. That mismatch has puzzled me ever since I was a child.

Yet the more I learned about the *tsubaki*, the more these two disparate things—the tree and the oil—began to approach each other in proximity. When you apply the principles of the Japanese language, you realize that *ra* and *ba* are generally interchangeable: hence *tsubaki* equates to *tsuraki*. Another linguistic rule says that *ru* and *ra* are interchangeable, as well: *tsura* thus basically means the same thing as *tsuru*. *Tsuru*—as in *tsurutsuru* (smooth)—is a mimetic word that basically means "smooth as a baby's bottom."

In short, the premodern Japanese saw the *tsubaki*—derived from the two words *tsuru* (smooth, by way of *tsuba* and *tsura*) and *ki* (tree)—as a tree with a perfectly smooth (*tsurutsuru*) surface. Its thick evergreen leaves have an unmistakable sheen (*tsuya*); even its trunk is smooth and hard. Its hard fruit, too, is plump, giving its surface a *tsurutsuru* burnish. The word for the tree—*tsubaki*—is evidently a kind of celebration of the camellia's *tsurutsuru* qualities.

In this light, you can understand how the *tsubaki* and *tsubaki-abura* (camellia oil) do, in fact, match up. Plants have always existed in close connection with humans thanks to their practical value. The expression for *tsubaki* is a perfect reflection of that intimacy.

The Japanese of old initially came up with the name *tsubaki* from its *tsuru-*

つらつらつばき

tsuru smooth texture that seemed to offer ample oil for humans to extract for their use, and so forged an intimate connection with the *tsubaki* tree by extracting its oil (*abura*). But they were also captivated by the pristine gloss (*tsuyayakasa*) of the tree's fruit. In Book 20 of the *Man'yōshū*, there is an "ode of praise," or *homeuta*, by the great poet Ōtomo no Yakamochi.[4] In the poem, the speaker declares to his lover that he wishes he could gaze "long and deep (*tsuratsura to*) upon your perfectly smooth body, as smooth as the *tsubaki*." The adverb *tsuratsura to* expresses the *tsubaki*'s glossy sheen, and also carries the meaning "thoroughly" and "sufficiently." These two words appear in quick succession, serving as pivot words (*kakekotoba*). *Tsuratsura* is synonymous with *tsubaraka*, which resembles the word *tsubaki* in terms of its sound. Ultimately, the poem stands out for its use of *tsuratsura* as a *kakekotoba* and the way it compounds the *tsubaki*'s visual beauty with emotion.

The poet can see the entire upright standing figure of the addressee—his lover called "you" (*anata*) in the poem—whose beauty he likens to the entire figure of the *tsubaki*. That's because the *entire* tree—and not just its flower—is *tsuratsura* smooth.

Tsuratsura tsubaki has a pleasant ring, its rhythm almost musical. When our ancestors used the word to praise the *tsubaki* tree's impressive figure (Book 1 of the *Man'yōshū*), the word lifted their spirits. The word would put those who heard it in a similarly joyous mood as well.

There are few plant names that contain such a keen awareness of the plant's beauty. From now on, shall we, too, call that tree the *tsuratsura tsubaki*?

4. Ōtomo no Yakamochi (ca. 718–785)

141

Hikobae
■ Fresh Shoots from Tree Stumps

When I visited the Kitayama area of Kyoto the other day, I encountered a number of Japanese cedar (*sugi*) stumps. I wondered how long it must have taken for the diameter of those stumps to reach one meter. I visualized an eternity of vigorous young saplings shooting up and the maternal body-like parent roots continuously generating them, year after year after year.

The shoots that develop from this parent root are what we call *hikobae*, which refers to the kind of bud that springs out of the parent root as a kind of "grandchild," or *hiko* in Japanese. The word *hiko* also connotes "descendant" or "offspring," which suggests that *hikobae* refers to buds that spawn generation upon generation of children. The ever-aging parent stump and the fresh, young growing buds seem to embody the lifecycle of nature, a process that stretches over the never-ending passage of time.

When I was a child, the awesome sight of an old parent tree root sprouting forth young *hikobae* shoots was quite the thing to behold. The *hikobae* of plum trees, for example, were especially captivating. The plum tree's proud, dignified posture hinted at why the Chinese literati poets and artists of classical antiquity held it in such high regard; pruned, the plum tree reveals a striking figure, with its crooked, winding form—an image that may very well have something to do with the well-known expression "It is stupid to prune cherry trees, but it is stupid not to prune plum trees" (*sakura kiru baka, ume kiranu baka*). The impressive figure of the plum tree with its winding branches also provides a stark contrast to its small, straight *hikobae.*

These days, I am smitten by the fresh *hikobae* shoots that grow from the stock of the century-old *kurogane* holly (round leaf holly) tree in my garden. The stock has spots that burst with young *hikobae* shoots and others that look positively spent. From those healthy, sprightly parts come young *hikobae* "grandchildren," sprouting fresh green leaves in a lush display of life.

Seeing those buds, I always marvel at how intuitive our predecessors were in calling the buds "grandchildren." Humans can give birth only to children, one generation at a time. But trees, to our ancestors, spawned grandchildren—a generational leap.

One might, of course, just as easily counter that, no, no, technically, the buds are not genetic offspring but rather just normal shoots. Such arguments, however, do not accord with the intuitive sense of it all.

The mystery of that old, doddering *kurogane* holly tree in my garden is how it keeps producing generation after generation of fresh young sprigs despite its advanced age. Its trunk—which appears withered beyond recovery—suddenly bursts forth with new life, as if by divine miracle. Its slender *hikobae* themselves capture the sheer joy that our ancestors must have felt when they looked on those slender shoots, their sprouts bursting forth into the world. People these days rarely show interest in the actual workings of the natural world, but the premodern Japanese were deeply connected to nature—they even created an entirely new word out of the generational impossibility of the "birth" of a grandchild. No doubt the great modern poet Kitahara Hakushū would have called it "a perfectly natural thing of this world—yet so unworldly as well!" (*nanigoto no fushigi nakeredo*), as he put it in his poem "Bara" (Two Songs for a Rose).

Hikobae

ひこばえ

Fujinami
Wisteria Blossoms Swaying in the Breeze

The Japanese wisteria—*fuji* in Japanese—is a species of flowering plant that Japanese people encounter regularly in their daily lives. The plant, characterized by its vine-like nature, doesn't stand out as a singular presence; rather, it extends by coiling itself around other plants, dangling down its long tufts of drooping flowers.

The flower clusters that hang from the wisteria—*hanabusa* 花房—are beautiful in the way they sway in the breeze, particularly when they are trained on horizontal trellises. *Fujinami*, which literally translates as "wisteria waves," is a metaphor likening that swaying motion to the undulations of ocean waves.

This metaphorical description *fujinami* has a history that spans over 1,300 years, dating back to the *Man'yōshū* (Book 3, among others). There have always been people who mistakenly read the word *fujinami* literally as the name of a plant. But let's be absolutely clear: the expression is, in fact, poetic through and through.

In 1994, I had the honor of serving as the composer of a poem (*meshiudo)* for the annual Utakai Hajime (first poetry reading) held at the Imperial Palace. The theme (*dai*) for the poetry at the gathering was the word *nami*—"wave." Normally, the simple poetic depiction of a wave would make for rather uninspired poetry. Since the imperial New Year's poems are presented to His Majesty the Emperor, I thought I would make my poem a so-called "ode" (*shōka* 頌歌). I decided to coin a new word: *sakuranami*, which equates to a "cherry-blossom wave."

Of course, cherry trees, or *sakura*, do not dangle their flowers the way *fuji* do. Nevertheless, they do send their petals scattering in a flurry with each gust of wind. The Japanese language has a term for that scattering: *hanafubuki*, or "flower blizzard," for cherry-blossom petals falling in the wind. In my poem, then, I tried to evoke the way flowers look as they ride a gust of wind, whirling and dancing as they move through the air. I imagined my *sakuranami* phrasing as a kind of mimetic invocation of the old wisdom so evident in the exemplary word *fujinami*.

When the wind blows, the wisteria's flower tufts lift and sway, making a kind of wave that gracefully crests and falls. How did the Japanese of antiquity regard that graceful movement? In fact, the lily flower is called *yuri* in Japanese because it flutters and sways (*yureru*) in a lilting, *yura-yura* way in the breeze; *yura* inspired *yuri*, and that swaying is what prompted the premodern Japanese to revere the *yuri* as a "holy flower," or *seika* 聖花. Moreover, an episode in Book 2 of the *Kojiki* describes a scene in which several aristocrats try to cure the taciturn imperial prince—who showed no signs of speaking despite his age—of his chronic reticence by putting him into a boat and rocking it to and fro, *yura-yura*, in order to get him to speak.

In the same way, they must have regarded the ever-swaying Japanese wisteria as a "sacred flower" (*seika*).

Moreover, the wisteria dons a splendid cloak of pale purple flowers. Purple— *murasaki* in Japanese—is one of the *shigoku-iro* colors that high-court officials wear on formal occasions. The color has long been a symbol of nobility.

With those images and associations in mind, Japanese people have used the word *fujinami*—with its rich nuances—for countless generations. The flowers, gently swaying in the breeze, indeed strike a noble, lofty air, a grace that resonates on *fujinami*'s distinctive linguistic wavelength.

Fujinami

ふじなみ

Hisago
■ Gourd

isago is an old way to say *hyōtan* 瓢箪, the Japanese word for the calabash gourd. Another way to express the same thing is *fukube.*

When a single thing has multiple names in Japanese, the word often has a diverse background.

The routes by which items of foreign origin came to Japan were generally via maritime channels, via the Chinese mainland, and via the Korean peninsula. It is impossible to say for certain which of these three routes the calabash gourd (*hyōtan*) traveled on its way to Japan. It'd be nice if the answer would just pop out of a gourd one day, out of the blue, but I doubt that would ever happen.

Setting the *hyōtan* gourd's route of entry aside, what we do know is that few plants have commanded the kind of esteem that the *hyōtan* has.

Split the gourd in half, and it can become a *shakushi* dipping ladle; use it in its entirety, as is, and you can fill it with *sake* or water.

Hollow out its insides, and you'll find that it floats without ever sinking. There's even that story in the *Nihon Shoki* about the man who defeated Ryūjin 龍神, the dragon god who wielded the power of the tides, by utilizing this special feature of unsinkability.

Another famous appearance of the *hyōtan* came on the flags of great daimyō warrior-general Toyotomi Hideyoshi[5]—the so-called "thousand gourd" (*sennari byōtan* 千成瓢箪) insignia. It may have been one that only he could have come up with, having made his way up in the world with a penchant for navigating human emotion.

I was recently surprised to find that stores have started selling plastic bottles shaped like *hyōtan* gourds. The middle, concave section of the gourd-like bottle

5. Toyotomi Hideyoshi (1537–1598)

I saw even had a string attached to it so that you could hang it from something, just as people used to do with *hyōtan* gourds. Those retro-themed containers were no doubt intended to evoke a sense of nostalgia for old Japan—a strategy that apparently worked well, as the bottles sold in high numbers.

The *hyōtan* gourd has had a prominent place in everyday life for years. In classical literature, it was known as *hisago*.

In Shinto mythology, there is a deity who lives at the watershed on a high mountain ridge. The deity possesses a "water-drawing gourd" (*kumihisago*), which it uses to draw the "water from heaven" (*ama-tsu-mizu*) and then send the water down the river, repeating the process ceaselessly. That's why river waters never run out. See Book 1 of the *Kojiki* for the account.

Book 2 of the *Kojiki* features another gourd-related episode. When a strong, feisty warrior-heroine of old had advanced her army across the sea, she floated *hisago* around the vessels—it was a magical spell to keep her troops afloat.

In *Sarashina Nikki* (Sarashina Diary, ca. 1059), the classic poetic diary from the Heian period, is an account of a popular song (*min'yō*) that appeared in eastern Japan. The song tells of a *hisago* gourd atop a large *sake* jar that changed its direction according to the wind's course. For instance, whenever the northern winds would blow, the *hisago* would point to the south.

Using the light, buoyant *hisago* as a kind of weathercock to gauge the movement of the wind, our forebears came to understand the seasonal changes, as well.

The *hisago* gourd has so many wonderful properties and a history so steeped in wisdom. It can even be used to catch the *namazu*, the mythological giant catfish that lives in the mud and causes earthquakes. What versatility!

Hisago

ひさご

Kinukatsugi
Steamed Skin-on Taros

Every time I think of it, I always enjoy the fact that little, round, potato-like taro roots, known as *satoimo* in Japan, also go by the name *kinukatsugi* (*kinu* 衣, or "clothing," and *katsugi* 被ぎ, or "wear" or "don").

The little round taro appears to be "clothed." It's a baby taro, after all, so it's bundled in soft baby clothes—or so the rendering goes.

Of course, you don't eat the baby's clothing—its skin, rather. Taro skin is not meant to be eaten; the root is best peeled. However, the traditional cooking method involves boiling it with its skin still on. You sprinkle a little salt into the boiling pot, wait for the taros to boil, and then finally peel and eat them.

If I may make an embarrassing confession, I never actually understood how the salty flavor gets inside the skin but not inside the taro. When I was a boy, I used to think it a tremendous waste to throw all that good salty taste away with the skin. I imagine I'm not the only one with that same confusion.

I often hear the complaint that people nowadays consume too much salt as it is. I am somewhat reluctant to accept this case against excessive salt intake. After all, people don't eat simply for the purpose of staying alive or maintaining perfect health. They eat food because it tastes good.

Nevertheless, I am aware that this little round root vegetable, taro, has the *kinukatsugi* name because you cook it with its "clothing" still on, which is why the light, salty flavor that seeps in through the skin tastes just right.

The cute, round taros are nice and gooey under the skin, accenting their delicious flavor.

き
ぬ
か
つ
ぎ

In Japan, there is a tradition of calling the *meigetsu*—the harvest moon on the fifteenth night of the eighth lunar month—by the name *imomeigetsu* (potato harvest moon) and dedicating *satoimo* taros as an offering to the moon. For Japanese people, the *satoimo*—more than any other type of tuber variety—carries the image of mountains, fields, and the taste of traditional homemade cooking.

Eventually, *kinukatsugi* and *imomeigetsu* both became haiku seasonal words (*kigo*) in the autumn classification.

There's another matter of critical importance. The correct way to say *kinukatsugi* is actually *kinukazuki*. *Katsugu*, the verb form of *katsugi*, means to hoist or shoulder a heavy object. On the other hand, *kazuku*, the verb form of *kazuki*, means to cover the head in clothing. Operating on that more correct foundation, the *kinukazuki* taro is swaddled in its skin as if it were donning a layer of clothing.

Long ago, there was a style of women's robe called the *kinukazuki* 衣被き, which women would put on over their heads to cover their faces. It's an exquisitely elegant piece of clothing, with its tasteful name vividly evoking a refined appearance. The similar name of the *kinukatsugi* root evokes that same type of elegance.

I propose that we call the *kinukatsugi* by its proper name: *kinukazuki*. The whole idea deserves the proper linguistic dressing, after all.

Hanasusuki

■ Japanese Plume Grass

Thesе days, the word *hana* (flower) appears after the name of the plant. So, for instance, we say *asagao no hana* (morning glory flower) and *yuri no hana* (lily flower).

In antiquity, however, the word *hana* would appear before the plant's name. Our ancestors would thus say *hana asagao* (flower morning glory), *hanayuri* (flower lily), and so forth.

I find this inverted phrasing a wonderful way to express the names of different flowers. In my lectures and classes over the years, I have always advised my audience to ask not for "*bara no hana*" (rose flowers) when they go to a flower shop but rather for "*hanabara*" (flower roses).

Isn't this expression far more beautiful than the usual modern way?

From this day forth, I implore you to adopt the original, reverse order. Speaking in beautiful phrases naturally beautifies our character, after all.

Hanasusuki is one such beautiful—and beautifying—word. The term comprises two distinct words: *hana*, or flower, and *susuki*, which means Japanese pampas grass.

Perhaps some people have never realized that Japanese pampas grass (*susuki*) does, in fact, have flowers. Small and numerous in number, the flowers look as if they've been sprinkled over the plant. From a distance, the *susuki* plant appears to be enveloped in a red tint, giving off a youthful glow—the sign that the flowers are in bloom.

As autumn deepens and winter approaches, the *susuki* plants come into full ear and eventually turn completely white. At this point, they start to become fluffy and eventually scatter about randomly, leaving the withered pampas grass

はなすすき

called *karesusuki*, or dried *susuki*.

If you give a *susuki* plant a close look, you can see the tiny, half-hidden flowers dotting the blades. It's an experience to enjoy—and the fact that we call it the *hanasusuki* reveals how closely our ancestors observed nature. That subtle sense of discovery, I think, makes the word even more delicate and exquisite than other *hana*-prefixed words such as *hanashōbu* (Japanese water iris) and *hanatsubaki* (camellia flower), whose flowers are flaunted openly in full view.

In antiquity, the *susuki* was known by another name as well: *obana* 尾花 (literally, "tail flower"). Because its long blades resembled animal tails, the plant was dubbed the *o no hana*, which literally means "flower with a tail," hence spawning the word *obana*. When you call the plant *obana*, you might start to see it as a kind of animal "tail" (*o* 尾). But when you call it *hanasusuki*, you focus more on the flower—and perceive it as such.

Evidently, the *susuki* acquired its name from the fact that its leaves and stalk stand up at a straight, sharp angle. Long ago, people would make thatched roofs using the *susuki*. Since the plant served a practical purpose as a building material, there wasn't any need to append the *hana* suffix; therefore, it just went by the name *susuki*.

In contrast to the *susuki*, with its building-material associations, the *obana* rendering of the *susuki* species makes it part of the so-called "seven autumn flowers" (*aki no nanakusa*). In Book 10 of the *Man'yōshū*, pampas grass appears as *obana* so often that it rivals the Japanese bush clover flower (*hagi*) in number of references throughout the work. The *hanasusuki* certainly won the hearts of our ancestors.

Hikarakuyō
Whirling Petals and Falling Leaves

The word *hikarakuyō* 飛花落葉 is a compound phrase that combines two Chinese words: *hika* 飛花 (whirling petals) + *rakuyō* 落葉 (falling leaves).

The first half of the term, *hika* 飛花, refers to flower petals fluttering about in the air. The idea has roots in the image of a cherry tree (*sakura*) in the process of losing its petals. The *rakuyō* 落葉 part of the word, meanwhile, connotes what happens when a rain shower comes sweeping in and causes leaves to fall from trees—a phenomenon that occurs in a wide variety of deciduous species.

The *hika* part denotes a natural occurrence that transpires in spring, but the *rakuyō* process most often takes place in autumn. In terms of scenic imagery, however, the two words actually refer to the same phenomenon. *Hikarakuyō* is a phrase that attempts to capture the whirling, falling movement itself, in its essence—not with a seasonal specificity.

In the interval between summer—when natural life flourishes with an ascending vivacity—and winter—when life quiets down—there is a short spell of natural variation that reshapes the fundamental state of life. *Hikarakuyō* speaks to that transformative dimension.

Our ancestors attached tremendous importance to seasonal change. The fluttering petals can be distracting and disorienting—so dangerous, in fact, that they can even get you killed. That is certainly how it seemed to Ōtomo no Yakamochi, whose poem on the subject appears in Book 17 of the *Man'yōshū*:

Yo no naka wa	When you count the world,
kazu naki mono ka	does it then add up to nothing?
haru hana no	For if one must die
chiri no magai ni	amid the flickering swirl of bloom
shinu beki omoeba	when the petals of spring flowers fall.[6]

6. See note 4 on page 301

In modern literature, it was Sakaguchi Ango[7] who echoed that same notion in his acclaimed short story "Sakura no mori no mankai no shita" (In the Forest, Under Cherries in Full Bloom, 1947).

In a similar way, falling leaves (*rakuyō*) have also inspired feelings of danger and peril. The classical poet Kakinomoto Hitomaro, for instance, grieved for his wife when she failed to return after wandering into the autumn hillsides and getting lost in the thick autumn leaves called *momiji*. Even today, many of us probably sense the beckoning of death in the image of fallen leaves. The image of incessantly falling leaves can be thoroughly mesmerizing.

In any event, the inclination of Japanese people to regard wanderings (*magire*) and confusion (*magai*) as dangerous hazards is a tradition that goes back a long way. The fact that people of the Heian period even referred to the vicissitudes of romantic love as "things in a state of disarray" (*mono no magire*) is a case in point.

In fact, many Heian-era people believed that the reason people fell in love was due to a certain mental disorder, a psychological disturbance.

Ironically enough, it was while living in the United States that the imagery and implications of fallen leaves struck me most profoundly. The trees along the boulevard, fanned by the strong winds, seemed to convulse as their leaves blew off in all directions. Meanwhile, along the road, huge piles of fallen leaves accumulated in massive heaps.

"That's it!" I found myself thinking, "*Hikarakuyō*—whirling petals and falling leaves!"

The great *renga* poets of the Muromachi period (1336–1573) valued the four-character *hikarakuyō* compound as a singularly poetic expression. In fact, the term had drawn substantial attention even further back in antiquity. Moreover, the phrase represents a scene that is found not only in Japan but also all over the world.

---

7. Sakaguchi Ango (1906–1955)

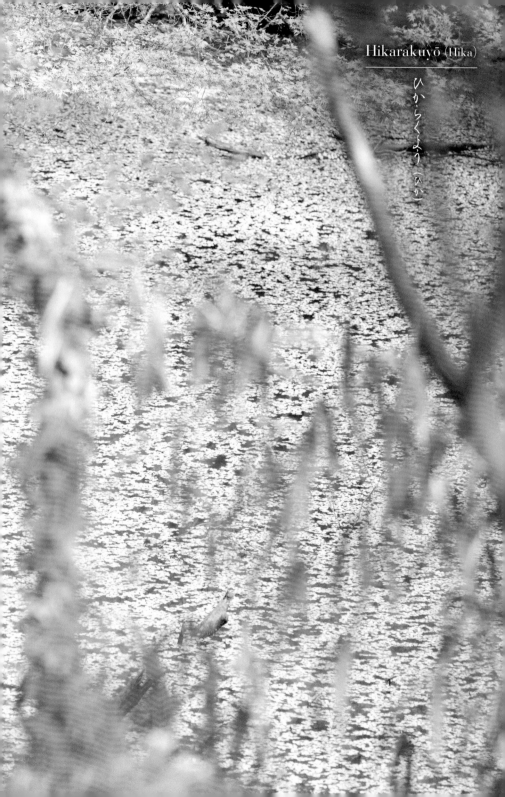

Hikarakuyō (Hika)

ひ・か・ら・く・よ・う（ひか）

Hikarakuyō (Rakuyō)

ひからくよう（らくよう）

Ubatama
■ Pitch-Black, Nocturnal

*U*batama is the term for the plant we now call *karasu-ōgi*, or "blackberry lilly" in English. In Chinese characters, it is written with 烏 *karasu* (crow) and 扇 *ōgi* (folding fan). The term, also pronounced *nubatama* on occasion, appears in classical literature as early as the *Kojiki* (Book 1) and has been in habitual use ever since—especially as a qualifier for describing night.

How on earth did the plant called *karasu-ōgi* become an epithet for evoking the images of pitch-black night?

Karasu-ōgi has leaves that open out flat, like a fan (*ōgi*), as they unfold. The ends of its branches grow red flowers. But when you pluck its fruit in autumn, you can see that the seeds are actually little round, black balls a mere three or four millimeters in diameter.

These particle-like pieces of fruit, appearing almost to have a black-lacquer finish, resemble little black beads—in a way, little black souls, or *tama* 魂. That's why *ubatama* is sometimes written as black bead or crow bead. The *karasu* of *karasu-ōgi*, too, comes from its real color: the so-called *karasu-iro*, or "crow color."

The plant itself gets its name from the mysterious quality of its fruit. To this extent, our forebears treasured the fruit—a veritable black spirit—for that very quality.

It is only natural, then, that *ubatama* should come to symbolize the pitch-black sense of mystery that permeates the dark night. You might even wonder if the *ubatama* could be the spirit of night itself.

A *waka* poem from the *Kojiki* (Book 1) expresses the transition from day to night as follows:

nubatama no	Gem-black
yo wa idenamu	the night emerges

The soul (*tamashii*) of the sentient night, the fruit of the *karasu-ōgi* dwelled in the wild grass. In this poem, the night is treated as a sentient being. As that living night's soul, the thing that dwelled in the wild grass was the fruit of the *karasu-ōgi*. Here, the poem anthropomorphizes the night in the phrase *yo wa idenamu*, literally "night emerges."

Naturally, in the nights of the distant past, there were no artificial lights. The premodern Japanese must have been full of fear, awe, and supplications for peace in the presence of night, whose soul they envisioned in the form of the *ubatama*—fragmented pieces of the nocturnal spirit.

In the West, the dandelion, or *tanpopo* in Japanese, is sometimes described as a fragment of sun fallen to Earth. In that sense, the inspiration for the word *ubatama* could have been a shard of the night, crumbling off and spilling earthward.

Years ago, I once brought some *ubatama* fruit to a meeting with a foreign audience.

"Would you like to try one of my *ubatama* fruit?" I asked the assembly.

In the blink of an eye, every last one of these "souls of sentient night" vanished from my hand into the palms of all those present.

Fūchisō

■ The Weathervane Plant

Just after the Second World War, revolutionary Marxist and author Miyamoto Yuriko[8] published her novel *Fūchisō* (The Weathervane Plant, 1946). I was initially attracted by the novel's (and plant's) beautiful name—*Fūchisō* 風知草, a seasonal word classified under summer—which literally means "grass that knows the wind" (*kaze o shiru kusa* 風を知る草), even though I had never actually seen the plant. Later, when I saw the plant for the first time, I was struck all the more by its strange beauty, with its long slender leaves. The *fūchisō*, otherwise known as the *urahagusa* (*ura* 裏 backside + *ha* 葉 leaf + *kusa* 草 grass), grows leaves whose front and back sides are flipped, so it seems—the leaf's white backside appears facing upward. It comes out looking as though the wind has played some mischievous trick on it. You might think that the long, slender plant simply surrenders itself up to the wind, spending its whole life fluttering about at the mercy of the wind's mercurial whims.

The word *kazamidori* 風見鶏, which refers to the weather vane or weathercock, literally means "cock that sees the wind": *kaze o miru tori* 風を見る鶏. The idea of a "wind-seeing fowl" has a bit of a humorous charm to it, in both how it looks and how it functions. I would venture to say that *fūchisō*, too, has a similarly endearing quality; we might take a cue from the *kazamidori* "wind-observing cock" and call it *kazamigusa* 風見草, or "wind-observing plant" (*kaze o miru kusa*). There is, of course, an actual tree called the *kazamigusa*: the plum tree

---

8. Miyamoto Yuriko (1899–1951)

(*ume*) sometimes goes by that name because people "detect" the course of the wind by gauging the intensity of upwind plum flowers' scents. The *fūchisō*, however, marks the strength of the wind by the way it sways. It also points out the path of the wind. It is probably that sensitivity to the wind, a kind of delicate receptivity, which earned the plant the name *fūchisō*. The name *fūchisō*, therefore, has a more winning charm than the name *urahagusa* does—its nuances betray a more knowing perception.

These days, I love to look at the lone *fūchisō* in a basin in my garden. But for all the supple pliancy of its leaves, it still manages to shoot forth a resilient ear with a distinctive splash of purplish color to accompany the green.

Miyamoto Yuriko no doubt likened her experience to that of the *fūchisō*. The novel describes her life amid the dizzying changes of the interwar and immediate postwar period, reflecting her pliancy in the face of fickle transformations with a remarkable sensitivity and attention to detail.

There is also another Japanese expression *kaze ni soyogu ashi* that likens something to the reeds (*ashi*) blowing in the wind (*kaze*).

But analogizing an experience to the luxuriant *fūchisō*, both in terms of the form the term evokes and the dignity in connotes, makes it a metaphor of a markedly higher order.

Hōzuki

Chinese Lantern Plant

The plant known in Japan as the *hōzuki* (Chinese lantern) goes strikingly well with *yukata*, or casual summer kimono. For me, the *hōzuki* is a signature sight of summer in the old *shitamachi* district of Edo, now the eastern part of present-day Tokyo. In summer, the *hōzuki* market around Sensōji Temple in the Asakusa district would get going; the small, round, red fruit would start showing up here and there and everywhere about town. On a certain day in autumn, the fruit would ripen to a red glow. Once the *hōzuki* has turned this red, you can see from the autumn skies that it's autumn.

One theory holds that the plant's name, *hōzuki*, comes from the word's literal meaning of *hō* (cheeks) + *tsukidasu* (to stick out). This suggests that people used to pop the fruit's seeds and blow into the fruit to make it sing. The second theory holds that the plant got its name from the fact that its fruits resembled the shape of a person's cheek: *hōtsuki*. Whatever its origin, we do know that the word has always been associated with young girls. As such, both the word's connotations and the fruit's actual appearance are indeed beautiful. Surely enough, the word eventually entered the classical lexicon as a metaphor for a beautiful female face.

In its *kanji* form, *hōzuki* is a combination that adds an ominous, mysterious dimension to the word's nuances: *oni* 鬼 (demon) and *akari* 灯 (light, lamp). I sometimes find myself entertaining the thought that the *hōzuki* might in fact be lights that hidden demons turned on in the fields but forgot to turn off.

Long ago, the *hōzuki* went by the name *kagachi*—a word that happens to appear in the allegory of the eyes of a large snake. The word *yamakagachi* (*yama* + *kagachi*) also happens to be the word for the largest snake in Japan; the bright red fruits may have been thought to be the eyes of that great serpent. At the same time, Japanese people used to call the *karasu-ōgi* plant (blackberry lilly) the *uba-tama*, which, as I explained on page 164, originally meant "jet-black, nocturnal gem-soul," because it has black seeds. Hence it is conceivable that the *kagachi* plant, in response to this, was called the bright red soul.

Long ago, people also wrote the name of the plant with the three Chinese characters 洛 (Luo River) + 神 (god) + 珠 (gem), which means the "goddess's gem on the Luo River." From this, we can see that the *hōzuki* plant was also considered to be a gem in the possession of a Chinese female deity who lived in the famous Luo River. The *oni* demon's firelight is no doubt one such fantastical story, as well.

The *hōzuki* was considered the gem of the female deity, the eye of the great snake, and the firelight that the *oni* demons would light—and they eventually became the playthings for young girls. It is therefore great fun to indulge in whimsical daydreams about the long, fantastical history of this red fruit.

Hōzuki

———

ほおずき

Sasanaki
■ Warbler Songs

*S*asanaki is the name for the faint song of the young bush warbler, called *uguisu* in Japanese. This term *sasanaki* is sometimes rendered as *sasa* 笹 (bamboo grass) + *naki* 鳴き (cry). If you're going to write it with Chinese characters, though, I'd say *sa* 小 (small) + *sa* 小 (small) + *naki* 鳴き (cry) is probably the better fit.

In Japanese, there's a rule that says we must distinguish between *sasa* and *saza*. *Sasa* is used to express small things, while *saza* is used to express large things. This is a rather ingenious method of differentiation if you ask me, as it creatively uses *nigori* (voiced) and non-*nigori* (non-voiced) phonetics to distinguish the relative size of something.

The soft, secret words between lovers are called *sasayaki*, which translates as "whispers." The raucous laughter that resounds through a crowded venue, however, is *warai-sazameki*. Likewise, *sasanami no* (細波の)—a "pillow word" (*makura kotoba*) epithet for the old Ōmi province—is the correct reading of the word, rather than "*sazanami.*"

The fact that *sasanaki* (warbler song) is written with *sasa* rather than *saza* implies that the bush warbler is still a small, young bird with underdeveloped vocal chords capable of making little more than a feeble cry. In short, the term *sasanaki* perfectly expresses the sound of the bush warbler.

In early spring, the bush warbler can only voice the faint cry of *chee-chee, chee-chee*. Right now, incidentally, I happen to be living at the foot of a mountain, which allows me to spend the spring days getting a firsthand grasp of all the goings-on in the life of the bush warbler. The way the bird modifies its song as it matures is a pleasure to observe.

Sasanaki is also a seasonal word (*kigo*), classified under winter. The word evokes the deep of winter, long before there are any hints of the coming of spring.

The bush warbler is said to fly away to remote villages in winter and then return to the valley when spring arrives. From the bird's seasonal movements, humans were able to discern that spring had come. People even developed the custom of calling the warbler the *haru-tsuge-tori*, which literally means bird (*tori*) that announces (*tsuge*) the advent of spring (*haru*).

While the seasonal connotations fall into the winter classification, *sasanaki* has also come to symbolize the "spring" of human life. Throughout the grueling winter, the bush warbler patiently awaits the arrival of spring, perched atop its withered winter branch. Then, you start to wonder when it might start singing:

Kudarano no	Will he have sung now—
hagi no furue ni	the warbler I saw perching,
haru matsu to	waiting for springtime,
orishi uguisu	on the old bush-clover branch
nakinikemu kamo	at Kudarano meadow?[9]
	Yamabe no Akahito[10]

This *tanka*, which appears in Book 8 of the *Man'yōshū*, contains a hidden metaphor: the poet has made it through hard times and now anxiously looks forward to the moment when the "flowers" of his life might start to blossom.

In the tones of the verses, you can almost hear the warbler's faint *sasanaki* song, a small, almost plaintive voice.

The fact that the premodern Japanese heard the warbler's cry as *ho-hokekyo* also speaks to the historical connection between humans and birds. The notably similar-sounding *Hokekyō* (*Lotus Sutra*) is, of course, one of the foundations of Buddhism, the principal text by which humans seek to attain salvation. By listening to and intoning the warbler's cry of *hokekyō*, then, people who were otherwise unable to chant the Buddhist *hokekyō* or visit a Buddhist temple could forge a bond with the Buddha in hopes of achieving liberation from the cycle of birth and rebirth.

---

9. See note 5 on page 301   10. Yamabe no Akahito (fl. 724–736)

Sasanaki

ささなき

Yana

■ Bamboo Fish Trap

Yana is a fishing instrument that catches fish swimming up and down a river and drops the haul into a basin, or *su* 簀.

Yana seem to have been developed way back in antiquity: the term appears in early classical texts, including the *Man'yōshū* (Book 3, among others). There's another expression, *ukawa o tate*, which refers to a method of snagging sweetfish (*ayu*) in the water by releasing trained cormorant birds (*u*) to catch the fish.

Fishing techniques employing cormorant birds apparently came to Japan from southern China, likely the same route that the *yana* technique followed at around the same time.

Summer is the peak season for *yana* fishing. When you think about how the *yana* system of catching large amounts of fish works, it can seem rather ruthless. However, it has its own quaint elegance, or what we call *fuzei*. When you see the *yana* wires in the river at summer's end, you see the remnants of the *yana*—the last vestiges of the busy summer fishing season, a feature of the late summer among the mountains.

Similarly, there is a fishing method called *ajirogi*, which involves catching fish by driving poles for wickerwork traps into the water to restrict the movement of fish. This method is used during winter, a mechanism for snagging the juvenile *ayu*, or *hio*.

In her classic work *Makura no Sōshi*, Sei Shōnagon notes that the use of *aji-rogi* in spring is "discordant"—by which she means that it is off-putting, out of harmony with spring. My impressions of off-season *yana*, however, are not as negative as hers.

On the contrary, the oddly quiet, vestigial *yana* wires seem to be more a part of the natural order than the *yana* bustling with hauls of fish could ever be.

But this may also be because the *yana* method is a comparatively relaxed fishing technique. While staying up north near the city of Sapporo in Hokkaido, I once spotted devices set in a river that served to catch salmon swimming upstream to lay eggs. The traps, which took up the whole breadth of the river, worked like this: boards in the water would narrow the spaces where the fish could swim upstream. The salmon would swim into the spaces, rotating a water-wheel-like structure, and then get trapped in the chambers, depositing them on the boards as the wheel turned. The technique was a method used by the indigenous peoples of North America, I learned.

My hope is that people will associate the fishing weir called the *yana* with summer and all its attendant sights; and that they will distinguish it from those modern machines and devices that are designed solely to kill fish in mass quantities.

Dedemushi

■ Snail

S trangely enough, the snail, or *katatsumuri* in Japanese, is also known by several other names: the *maimai*, *dedemushi*, and *maimaitsuburo*, to name a few.

The name *dedemushi* is sometimes alternately pronounced *dendenmushi*, a diminutive rendering that makes the creature even more childlike and endearing. There's a traditional children's song whose refrain goes,

> *Dendenmushi mushi, katatsumuri* Snail, snail, where is your head?
> *Omae no atama wa doko ni aru?* Stick out your horns, stick out your spear,
> *Tsuno dase, yari dase, atama dase!* Stick out your head!

The *denden* part of *dendenmushi* may have come from this verb *dasu* repeated in the refrain, "*Tsuno dase, yari dase, atama dase!*"

At the same time, you scarcely have to touch a snail to see it suddenly curl up; all that remains is the shell, a curious whorl.

You might find yourself wanting to see the snail move around and "dance," too, which explains the name *maimai*—a phrase equating to "dance, dance!" As with *dedemushi*, the name calls to mind how one might command something to do a little jig: "*mae mae!*"

A popular song from the late Heian period, anthologized in the *Ryōjin Hishō*,[11] depicts a child trying to rally a snail to dance. The child beckons to the snail (*katatsumuri*) with the following chorus: "And if you dance beautifully, I will take you to the flower garden to play."

It's obviously too much to expect a snail to dance—which is what makes that

---

11. *Ryōjin Hishō* (Songs to Make the Dust Dance on the Beams, compiled 12th c.)

で
で
む
し

image so appealing. There are few things as captivatingly illusory, as imagination-stirring as the thought of that quiet little creature lifting itself up to perform the *maimai* dance.

Just what compelled our forebears to come up with such a wild, fanciful notion? Did they find in that image of the slow, slimy creature, lugging around its heavy shell, moving only in sluggish, circular patterns, the very image of themselves?

I'd imagine that the *katatsumuri*, too, surely harbors a secret longing to dance about beautifully amid a wild profusion of blooming flowers—but all it can do is slowly inch its way through the world. It's the same for us, and even worse: it's not only that we can't dance to our heart's content, but our corporeal selves will likely meet their ends without so much as making a mark. We might not even have the chance to thrust out our own horns and spears.

When you reflect upon your own life in this way, the *katatsumuri* becomes an even more sympathetic and endearing figure. The fact that we feel an emotional connection with the creature—regardless of whether we call it *maimai, dedemushi, maimaitsuburo*—reflects our feeling of unconscious affection toward it. Our affinity for the snail might also come from the fact that we can spot it even during the rainy season, when earth and sky are ripe with rain.

It was Kōda Rohan,[12] the great writer of the Meiji period, who named his home after this creature, calling it "Snail Cottage" (*Kagyūan*). Did Rohan consider himself a *dedemushi*, a natural recluse wary to emerge out into the world? Or did he fancy himself a *maimai*, ready to dance upon command?

---

12. Kōda Rohan (1867–1947)

Amenbō
Water Strider

*A*menbō almost certainly comes from the phrase *ame no bōzu*, which might be translated as "rain boy." Japanese have long showed a predilection for shortening the word *bōzu* to *bō* and then affixing it to the ends of proper nouns as a diminutive, softening suffix. *Amaenbō*, for instance, is the diminutive for a person who is emotionally dependent, pampered, and spoiled—in short, a person who tends to indulge in others' kindness (*amaeru*). Likewise, *kikanbō* refers to a spoiled brat who simply refuses to listen; *kikan* is a negative form of *kiku*, or "listen." *Amenbō* is simply another instance of this custom.

What the term *amenbō* signifies, however, is that small, spider-like animal that stretches its legs over the water and swiftly darts across the surface.

The confusing thing is that there is another little bug called the *mizusumashi* (whirligig beetle), which glides over the surface of the water in much the same way. *Mizusumashi* is simply an alternate name for the *amenbō*. In short, some *mizusumashi* are *amenbō*, but at the same time, some *mizusumashi* aren't—hence the confusion.

But what we're discussing here is the *amenbō* that resembles the spider. *Amenbō* are quite small—no longer than three centimeters—which gives them a rather cute physical appearance. The name *amenbō* seems to suggest that rain (*ame* 雨) has somehow transformed itself into a child (*ko* 子). If that were the case, I'd love to see *amenbō* appear in the puddles that remain after the rain has let up, to watch those *amenbō* "rain children" skip about on the water after a storm.

The fact of the matter, however, is that the Chinese characters used to write the word *amenbō* are 水 (*mizu*, or "water") and 馬 (*uma*, or "horse"). I find

あめんぼう

this choice of characters most amusing. I can imagine it now: a TV quiz show where the contestants are asked to pronounce this combination of characters—*mizu* 水 + *uma* 馬—only to struggle in vain trying to answer it.

"I know there's another word that combines *umi* 海 (sea) and *uma* (horse)," one guest might say, referring to *tatsu-no-otoshigo* ("seahorse" in English), "but this one beats me!"

"No, no!" a fellow contestant chimes in. "The characters for 'sea' and 'horse' make *kaiba* (海馬), the word for the hippocampus!"

Laying that contentious back-and-forth to rest, I, for one, find the characters for *amenbō* lovely. Given the *amenbō*'s small size, it's quite an exaggeration to use the character "horse" in its name. Then again, I can't be the only one who sees the parallels between the *amenbō* and the knights in the traditional Japanese board game *shōgi*—*keima* 桂馬, another compound featuring the character for horse. Both small and agile, the *amenbō* and *keima* have a swift celerity; the silky-smooth movements of the *amenbō* as it glides across the water are a pleasure to watch.

Moreover, the term *mizusumashi*—that *amenbō* alias—carries the connotation of something that "cleanses" or "purifies" (*sumasu* 清ます "to purify") the water (*mizu*). In fact, this small insect preys on smaller insects and, by moving the surfaces of ponds and lakes, helps clean the water. At any rate, merely watching these little bugs, these gifts from some divine spirit after a rain, is certainly a refreshing experience.

Higurashi
■ Evening Cicada

There seems to be a growing number of people who say that they no longer hear the buzzing cries of the cicada, or *semi* in Japanese. What a terrifying age we live in! Long ago, the cicada's drone (*nakigoe*) was regarded as *the* emblem of summer. In the modulations in the cicada's song, that quintessential summer sound, people would read the trajectory of the season.

The source of that raucous summer buzzing is a cicada known as the *minminzemi*, whose name is derived from its cry: *meen-meen*. Just hearing that piercing cry is enough to make the summer heat feel twice as hot. The same goes for the *aburazemi*, or large brown cicada. The droning cries of the *aburazemi* were constants throughout the summer vacations of my youth, its voice that cries *gee-gee* comes right around the end of the semester.

Then, another cicada joins the chorus: the *higurashi*, or evening cicada. Compared with the cries of *meen-meen* and *gee-Gee*, the *kana-kana* sound of the *higurashi* cicada, which voices its song in clear tones, has a pretty ring, its rises and falls sounding cool. The *higurashi*'s cry really does give you the sense that summer is ending and autumn is just around the corner; in haiku, reflecting that seasonal quality, *higurashi* is a seasonal word (*kigo*) in the autumn classification.

Of course, the advent of autumn isn't what causes the *higurashi* to sing. It simply sings as a product of its environmental conditions: autumnal temperatures, the right light, and the optimal heat levels. The fact that we call this cicada the "evening cicada" (*higurashi*) suggests that evening (*higure*) and dawn, for that matter, match perfectly with the *higurashi*'s essential nature and ecosystem.

These cadences and inflections of the *higurashi* evening cicada's melody, so cool and beautiful, mirror the environment of autumn itself. Autumn, too, with its limpid sunlight, perfectly matches the clarity of the *higurashi*—an inherent feature that differs markedly from those of the *aburazemi* and the *minminzemi*.

The name *higurashi*—which connotes the idea of something "darkening" (*kuraku suru*) the day (*hi*)—is tantamount to describing the species as an administrator of time, so to speak. I need not remind you that our ancestors used their natural ecosystems in place of calendars and clocks. But I relish the idea that they seem to have taken everything a step further and made the environment more than just a measure of time; they saw the inhabitants of nature even *advancing* time itself, from dawn to dusk.

The history of the term *higurashi* goes back to antiquity, as far back as the *Man'yōshū* (Book 15). The word appears in a poem by an impatient traveler aching to get back to his wife, whom he has left in his hometown. In modern poetry, too, the great poet Miyoshi Tatsuji wrote a poem called "Tsubame" (Swallow), which describes swallows conversing with one another about how they know that when the evening cicada (*higurashi*) cries, it's time to head south. It's a beautiful poem, capable of stirring such a palpable longing for home because of its use of the *higurashi* motif.

Akitsu
Dragonfly

The dragonfly—*tonbo* 蜻蛉 in Japanese—was once called by another name: *akitsu* (秋津).

Akitsu literally means *aki no mono*, or an "autumn thing," reflecting the fact that we see dragonflies in abundance when the season turns to autumn.

For many, the dragonfly conjures up memories of watching dragonflies hunting for insects in the summer. One of the strongest associations likely has to do with seeking out the red dragonfly, or *akatonbo*, which becomes prominently visible in the sky right around the start of autumn. In haiku poetry, the word *tonbo* is a seasonal word (*kigo*) for autumn.

Here, I should note something important about the poetic vocabulary of seasonal words (*kigo*). The word *yosamu*, for instance, which is written *yoru* 夜 (night) + *samu* 寒 (cold), is a seasonal word for autumn. Winter—not autumn—is obviously when most of us feel cold at night. However, the timing is just a bit different: we find ourselves shivering at night in the late autumn. The season when we physically notice that it's cold at night is, in fact, autumn, not winter.

The same goes for *yonaga*, another seasonal word for autumn, written with the Chinese characters *yoru* 夜 (night) + *nagai* 長 (long). *Hinaga* (日 for day and 長 for long) is a seasonal word for spring, meanwhile. So it goes with various other terms. The wonderful quality of these seasonal words (*kigo*) is their ability to organize the natural seasons according to our actual sensory perceptions without simply calculating seasons by day count.

Autumn is the season of the harvest. Accordingly, the dragonfly has long had symbolic connections to the harvest's bounty. It was treated as a special insect since early antiquity, dating as far back as the Yayoi period (third cen-

tury BCE–second century CE). The dragonfly was regarded as so special that it even appeared in the patterns of those richly decorated ancient Japanese smelted bronze bells known as *dōtaku*.

Of course, the dragonfly has also won our gratitude for feeding on the destructive insects that eat away at crops, too. They were so helpful to ancient humans that they even appear in the *Kojiki*: a poem in praise of Emperor Yūryaku[13] lauds the dragonfly (*akitsu*) for promptly eating the horsefly (*abu*) that had landed on his arm.

Moreover, there's a species of dragonfly called the *shōryō tonbo* 精霊蜻蛉— the "dragonfly of the spirits of the dead." The *shōryō tonbo* earned its name from the fact that it appears around the Obon Spirit Festival, also known as the Shōryō Festival, which is the main festival honoring one's ancestors, held mainly on the fifteenth day of the seventh lunar month. The Obon Spirit Festival is a 1,300 year-old Japanese Buddhist festival that honors the spirits of one's ancestors.

Come to think of it, as a boy, I was taught that all dragonflies were, in fact, *shōryō*—spirit apparitions of the dead. We learned that they were the apparitions of countless ancestors who had returned to their respective birthplaces to visit their living descendants.

Dragonflies have, over Japan's long history, held a special place in people's hearts; they represented the spirits of the dead (*shōryō*), returning home during the autumn harvest season. After all, the word that our ancestors used for the insect—*akitsu*, or "autumn thing"—created an association with an entire season and with people's devout faith. The red dragonfly retains some of that mystical quality for quite a few of us.

13. Emperor Yūryaku (418–479)

Akitsu

あきつ

Words about the Human Heart

Aratama

■ Uncut Gem

There are three Chinese characters for rendering the word *ara*: 荒, 粗, and 新. The first character connotes roughness; the second coarseness; and the third newness. All three are legitimate expressions for the word.

I can make the assertion that *ara* is etymologically the same word as both *aru* 在る (to be, to exist) and *aru* 生る (to live, to exist). These two *aru* types both denote the same thing: existence, presence, being. Furthermore, I can assert that *aratamaru* 改まる (to renew, to reform) and *arau* 洗う (to wash) are closely related verbs. In short, the traditional Japanese way of thinking on the issue of "being" is embedded in this cluster of words, starting with *aru* and *ara*. Allow me to elaborate.

When something is born, it possesses its own autonomous being. When an alteration occurs at some point within that being, its life force therein is renewed, updated.

In other words, an object or entity that has just come into being is often rough and ragged: *ara*, as we say. All things inevitably grow old in time. But when washed, they spring to life once again. This process of revitalization is precisely the meaning of *arau*: to cleanse and revive that which has deteriorated.

This fundamental ontological premise lies at the heart of the Japanese perspective on life.

The souls (*tamashii*) that dwell within this sort of life force are what we call *aratama*. The *tama* part of the word equates the soul's visible form to either *tama* 玉 (gem) or *tama* 珠 (pearl). The distinction between these two types of *tama* is their place of origin: the former is found in mountains, the latter in the ocean. Perhaps you may have thought that the human soul was in the shape of a heart,

but it was a sphere, a round, beautiful shape.

The soul grows and matures from time to time. *Nikitama*, the Japanese word for the "mature" soul, is a combination of the Chinese characters for "harmony" (和) and "soul" (魂). Crucially, Japanese people have always regarded themselves as possessing both types of spirit. When fighting, we possess an uncut gem of a soul, a blunt, rough spirit, an *aratama*. When the situation calls for conciliation, our harmonious soul—*nikitama*, serves this function.

Incidentally, Japanese people have long thought that the temporal unit called the year (*toshi*) is replaced with a new one when the new soul (*aratama*) comes around on a one-year cycle. This notion spawned the expression *aratama no toshi*, with *aratama* serving as a *makura kotoba*, or "pillow word." The word *toshi*, which means year, also means harvest. The one-time brand-new soul brings about a one-time brand-new harvest; then the brand new soul once again trades places with the new soul that brings forth once again the next harvest.

This, at least, is what our premodern Japanese ancestors thought about the matter. But in fact, as Romanian religion scholar Mircea Eliade[1] notes in his book *The Myth of the Eternal Return* (1949), several African tribes have held the same types of views—that each "year" unit coincides with the bearing of a new spirit-soul.

I see this flexible, reverent view of the spiritual world as one of the Japanese people's most wonderful possessions. And to think—the universality of the *aratama* idea extends all the way to Africa! The word has a pleasant ring, rich with overtones.

1. Mircea Eliade (1907–1986)

Tama-no-o

String of Beads

The power of the famous classical *waka* collection *Ogura Hyakunin Isshu* as an educational tool lies in its immensity. I first encountered the word *tama-no-o* in a poem from the collection, by the poet Princess Shokushi:[2]

Tama no o yo	Like a string of beads,
taenaba taene	break now—shatter, my life!
nagaraeba	For if I live on
shinoburu koto no	I must surely lose the strength
yowari mo zo suru	to conceal my secret love.[3]

Although at that time I learned that *tama-no-o* (string of beads) means life (*inochi*), it took me several decades to understand just why it had that deeper significance.

In short, *tama* denotes the same thing as the word *tamashii* 魂: "soul" or "spirit." *Tamashii* is a soul that lives forever. In classical Japanese, adding a *no o* to the end of a word meant that whatever the word referred to would continue in perpetuity. The term *tama-no-o* thus denotes a soul or spirit with an eternal existence.

It is important to stress that *tamashii* (soul) constitutes the kernel of a person's life force (*inochi*). By adding a *no o* to *tama* (=*inochi*), the word thereby came to express eternally continuing life.

No grade-schooler would ever understand this, surely.

But when you start to think about it, you can see how truly amazing the word *tama-no-o* is. First of all, the core of the life force is the soul (*tamashii*). This is a nice identification, a good place to start. The human body is just a *karimono*, which literally means both a temporary vessel and something borrowed. Hence,

---

2. Princess Shokushi (1149–1201) 3. See note 6 on page 301

when the soul leaves the vessel of a person's body, death descends upon the person. The modern verb *hanareru* 離れる, which means "to depart" or "to separate from," was read *kareru*—the same word for "to wither" or "to wilt"—in classical Japanese. *Hanareru* therefore meant the same thing as flowers wilting (*kareru*) and expiring, or losing their life force.

What happens, then, to the eternal soul (*tamashii*) when it "departs" from the body? In antiquity, people believed that the soul would become a bird once it had vacated its mortal flesh. When I explained this belief to a group of elementary students, one of them asked me, "So what happens when that bird dies?"

The bird, I answered, becomes the wind when it dies.

In this way, the soul exists for all eternity. The idea that the individual's life force (*inochi*) continues until the last breaths of the wind is worthy of our appreciation.

The body (*nikutai*) and its life force (*inochi*) are two distinct entities. When the soul leaves the body, the body becomes a leftover corpse, an empty nothingness, a *kūmu* 空無 as the Buddhists say. The body extinguishes itself in the process of the physical transformation we call death. In contrast, the soul constitutes none other than life itself: now turning to birds, now becoming wind. The process of dwelling anew in a different body is none other than the essence of the life force, or *inochi*. In Book 4 of the *Man'yōshū*, we find the following *waka* poem by the female poet Nakatomi no Iratsume:[4]

Tada ni aite	If only I could meet you
Miteba nomi koso	in the flesh
Tamakiwaru	and see you, only then
Inochi ni mukau	would longing cease its hold
Waga koi yamame	on my soul-swollen life.[5]

This *waka* boldly expresses the depth of the writer's love for another, a love that transcends temporal and spatial distances, stretching to the very last moments of the life force (*inochi*).

---

4. Nakatomi no Iratsume (fl. 8th c.)   5. See note 7 page 301

Misogi
■ Shinto Purification Ritual

The "wedded rocks" at Futamigaura in Ise, a pair of differently sized rocks linked by gigantic ropes, are believed to represent the progenitor gods of Japan, Izanagi and Izanami. But very few people know that on the summer solstice, the sun appears to rise from right in between those two rocks, as though it's emerging through a gate, and ascends directly over distant Mount Fuji.

I made a trip there one summer solstice several years ago at three a.m. in hopes of feasting my eyes on that spectacular sunrise. Unfortunately, due to the thick cloud cover, the sun disappeared as it rose from behind Mount Fuji over the horizon—but I was able to catch a brief glimpse of the sun breaking through and releasing its shafts of light from between the two rocks.

Since my trip coincided with the festival of the summer solstice, I did happen to see a *misogi*—Shinto purification ritual—taking place out in the middle of the ocean, which proved to be an even more valuable experience. Watching it all take place, I felt refreshed inside and out.

For over a millennium, Japanese people have performed *misogi* purification rituals in order to expunge the impurities of body and mind. If you consider

misogi from an academic standpoint, you find that the original meaning was to erode an object away by using water (*mizu de sogu*); the Japanese traditionally entrusted water with the task of washing away the filth and impurities (both literally and figuratively) that gathered on the body. They held the fervent, single-minded belief that impurity (*kegare*) was an accumulation of dirt or dust— or *aka*, as we say—and they selected water as a physical cleansing tool, not unlike the popular style of skin-exfoliating body scrubbing known as *akasuri* (literally, "grime scrubbing"). A Shinto *norito* prayer even references a belief in a certain deity, dwelling in the most distant reaches of the ocean, who swallows up the grime of human impurities washed away by the water.

Clearly, this long-held belief in the power of ablutions was a product of a sincere intent to atone for sins. At the same time, the Japanese of old accurately intuited what science now confirms about water's capacity to purify things; their faith in the power of water was not just some groundless superstition. I hope we continue to cherish the sentiments that previous generations poured into the *misogi* ritual and all the word's striking connotations.

Misogi

みそぎ

Tsuragamae
Countenance

The word *tsuragamae* is imbued with great power: even within the Japanese language, which abounds with delicate and subtle words, there are also words that possess an undeniable force. Simply the sound of the word *tsuragamae* is enough to bring a certain countenance to mind, a face turned this way, peering at you.

Moreover, the word conveys an expression so stealthy and cautious that you can feel the bold intensity and courage that lies behind the face.

Quite a few terms and phrases in Japanese relate to war and battle: the expression *ronjin o haru*, which means to set forth an argument as if in battle; *mato o ita kotae*, which denotes a succinct answer that hits the mark; the two old words for right and left hand—*mete* (rein hand) and *yunde* (bow hand), respectively, which have their roots in medieval warfare. Such words and phrases reflect an often-forgotten aspect of Japan, one markedly different from the popular images of the peace-loving nation and its people's harmonious, gentle character.

I always explain the apparent contradiction in the following way.

Japanese culture developed as a culture of sentiment—the often-cited *jō no bunka*—which formed within the framework of the sociopolitical order of the *kuge* (nobility) system that dominated the Japanese imperial court in Kyoto. This "culture of sentiment" has managed to survive to the present day—indeed, it constitutes the very core of Japanese culture. However, after the aristocratic *kuge* system declined and feudal samurai rule (*buke*) took over, the new system endorsed the warrior culture known as *bushidō*: the "way of the samurai." Many Japanese people today mistakenly believe that *bushidō* is Japanese culture in

つらがまえ

itself—but in fact, the older *kuge* system laid the groundwork.

The term *tsuragamae* played a key role in endorsing *bushidō seishin*, the "samurai spirit." About a decade ago, when I met a descendant of a feudal lord (*hanshu*) of a great domain of the Edo period, I was struck by his dignified countenance—that is, his *tsuragamae*—which suggested the mien of a samurai (*bushi*).

It is important to stress, then, that the *bushidō* credo does not simply valorize brute force for its own sake. It upholds a culture of strength, to be sure. But that strength rests firmly on the "culture of sentiment." The elite samurai *bushi* were not simply a class with the capacity for waging war. The famed expression *bushi no nasake*—which means "samurai tenderness"—reflects the reality that samurai were also capable of warm emotions.

The term *tsuragamae* emerged from the unfolding progression of dynamic cultural formation. The word was clearly never meant to denote the purely vicious or violent faces of those exclusively devoted to martial arts, those lacking the element of compassion. Nor was it a word that expressed the soft, elegant face of a fetchingly handsome young man.

The only face worthy of the *tsuragamae* name is one that possesses a dependable, individual self, a face that looks its opponent squarely in the eye, sending a penetrating gaze through clear, unclouded eyes.

The word bursts with strength—but true strength is something that is often hard for humans to recognize. The beauty of the word *tsuragamae* is a revealing glimpse into the beauty of that true strength.

Tsuragamae

つらがまえ

Omokage
■ Trace

Most people equate seeing an *omokage* of the dead, a kind of apparition or "trace" of a person, with witnessing the "form" (*sugata*) of
the deceased. The moment we describe *omokage* as "form" (*sugata*),
however, the nuance of the word changes, its mysterious resonance fading completely.

Initially, the word *omo* (face) referred to the principle (*omo na*) aspect—or
face—of a person. In other words, it signified the aspect of the person that represented the whole of his identity. The word *omote* therefore referred to all important existing things that humans associate with the face. In *jidaigeki* (historical
dramas) in film and on television, a feudal lord (*tonosama*) will often admon-
ish a subordinate with a common line: "There is no need for formalities—lift
your face!" (*kurushū nai, omote o ageyo!*). The subordinate's lowering of his face
(*omote*) signals deference. By giving the subordinate permission to lift his "face"
(*omote*), the feudal lord is essentially refusing gestures of obedience and allowing
the subordinate to "face" him directly. Accordingly, interactions involving the
concept of "face" become matters of human status.

The second half of *omokage*—*kage*—has a rather curious denotation.[6] In the
phrase *kage o otosu*, which means "to cast a shadow," for example, *kage* means
"shadow" or "silhouette." On the other hand, when you say the word *tsukikage*
(moonlight, moonbeams), you are referring not to a shadow but rather to the
"luminescence" (*hikari*) of the moon (*tsuki*). It might be hard to see how *kage*
can simultaneously mean one thing and its opposite. But what is light (*hikari*)
other than brightness that comes and goes, flickering on and off? When the lights

6. For my commentary on the term *kage*, see page 28

are on, *kage* signifies light. When the lights are off, *kage* indicates shadow.

Hence, we can say that *omokage* represents the essence (face) of a given person or thing illuminated.

As such, an *omokage* has a luminescent, radiant dimension. People don't say "Oh, what a hateful *omokage!*"

It is impossible to conceive of an *omokage* with such a negative nuance. About those we find detestable, we say things like "I feel nauseous just thinking about that scoundrel's ugly mug!" By contrast, when we use the word *omokage*, we are recalling that person or thing with a sense of nostalgia, a tinge of fond affection.

Put simply, the basic premise that underlies *omokage* in all its forms is none other than love—*ai* 愛 in Japanese.

In this light, you can see how sentiments are intimately intertwined with language and words. At the same time, however, you can also understand how we use language almost unconsciously, only vaguely aware of its contours.

When you think about it, then, you realize that we find certain words beautiful and pleasant precisely because they possess within them the very foundation of beauty and pleasantness.

Words contain the basis for beauty—and drawing on that inherent feature gives the things we write and say a richness, allowing beautiful words to do remarkable things for us.

Nonki

■ Carefree

Nonki is another word I am particularly fond of. The word connotes a quality that seems next to unattainable in our hustle-bustle contemporary world.

There's more to life than busying yourself with constant work. Once in a while, everyone wants to relax and be *nonki*. But what does that *nonki* really mean? Does *nonki*, written 呑気, simply mean wanting to go out for drinks—in short, *nomu* 呑む (to drink alcohol) + *ki* 気 (mood)? Is it *nonki* to drink all hours of the day? I think not.

Originally, *nonki* came from China. It was written with the two characters for "warm" (*dan* 暖) + "mood" (*ki* 気). This pronunciation of the character "warm" (*dan* 暖) as "*non*" falls into the special category of *tōon* 唐音, or pronunciations from the Song dynasty that made their way to Japan.

The most famous examples of *tōon* readings of Chinese characters are 行 as *an* (normally *gyō* but *an* in words such as *anka* 行火, bedwarmer, and *andon* 行燈, paper lantern) and 経 as *kin* (normally *kei* but *kin* in words like *kankin* 看経, silent reading of Buddhist sutras). In particular, these types of pronunciations abound in Buddhism-related terms.

Nonki also made its way to Japan around the same time that Buddhism did. And so, with its *tōon* pronunciation, *nonki* meant "a warm mood."

When you apply the word "warm" (*atatakai*)—written with the same character 暖 as the original *non* of *nonki*—to the weather, it both suggests warm temperatures and clement weather. Another word with connections to the word

nonki is *nōtenki* (能天気). *Nō* is the same *nō* 能 as brain (脳). And *tenki* 天気, or weather, not only denotes weather in general but also connotes "sunny weather." Therefore, *nōtenki* refers to "sunny weather" in the brain: a *nōtenki* person has a careless, happy-go-lucky demeanor. *Nonki* has a similar meaning.

However, *nonki* does not have any of the negative connotations that *nōtenki* possesses. With *nonki*, one's head and heart and body are all warm; one's mind is free of any hostile, biting thoughts; and one's attitude toward worldly matters is completely relaxed. Such a tranquil disposition allows one to see things as they are, to be generous of heart, and to perform benevolent deeds. With this attitude, one can learn empathy, as well.

People nowadays seem to regard *nonki* more and more as a kind of vice, a moral flaw. This, however, is a mistake—*nonki* is anything but. In the Taishō period, *nonkibushi*, or "*nonki* tunes," was a popular form of song. The author Ozaki Kazuo,[7] wrote fictional works such as *Nonki Megane* (Carefree Glasses, 1933), which won the Akutagawa Prize in 1937. From the Taishō period to the early Shōwa period, there was an economic collapse and depression, a sloping descent into militarism and war, and a "closing of the age" (*jidai heisoku*). It was no coincidence that *nonki* captured popular interest amid that widespread strife—a savior in the form of a single word.

In our modern age, often lamented as a spiritual wasteland, the notion of *nonki* deserves a resurgence—a carefree, laid-back attitude might be exactly what we need.

7. Ozaki Kazuo (1899–1983)

Nonki
のんき

Sabiru

◼ To Rust

"This knife has too much *sabi* on it—it won't cut!" Such laments are by no means rare. When *sabi*—"rust" in English—spreads through iron, the object becomes reddish brown and weathered, like an ancient iron sword unearthed from an ancient burial mound.

At the same time, there are many elegant Japanese words that contain the word *sabi*: *sabishii* (lonely) and *otomesabiru* (truly girlish) and *wabi-sabi*, which are terms found in the fields of haiku and *sadō* (tea ceremony).

In fact, you may be surprised to hear that these words are all synonymous with *sabi*—the rust that corrodes iron. A *sabishii fūkei* (lonesome landscape) is infused with *sabi*: it has acquired "rust." And what is so "girly" about a young girl is that she has acquired a kind of "rust." The quality of *sabi* in haiku poetry, too, is precisely the product of this preference for *sabi*.

And yet, considering the matter of *sabi* in this way enables us to feel some of the wonder of Japanese culture. The word *sabiru* used to be written with the character 然 (*sa biru* 然びる), which denotes the natural attributes or original nature of a thing: the thing as it is meant to be. The landscape is wholly natural and spontaneous, not at all forced, without affect or artificiality. It is the nature of young girls to be girlish, to be free of any unnaturally adult attributes. In haiku, too, the natural spontaneity of the form of the thing expressed is the perfection thereof. When it comes to iron, polishing and sharpening—a shiny glint—is not in the inherent nature of iron itself. Iron, by nature, is a substance that cannot withstand the corrosive power of acids; its true nature is to rust.

Since antiquity, Japanese people have always harbored a radical antipathy toward forced affectation and artificiality—*wazatorashisa* in Japanese. For example, the ideal old man is one who abides in a mode of *okinasabu*: behavior that one would naturally expect of an old man. That's why we do not extol the elderly for their youthful affectations and artificialities. In the same way, scenery-destroying, ugly modern buildings have no place in rusted, lonely *sabita* landscapes. The natural, scenic landscape is all that merits value.

Do you not find the rust of iron especially appealing? Since it is the nature of iron to rust, iron is not innately cut out for making weapons. But when you process iron into a sharp-edged instrument, it can become a tool for murder. Such wicked ideas, however, did not come natually to our ancestors. For them, rust was simply a benign attribute, a sign that an object had at last realized its true form.

I do not want to invite misunderstanding. It's not enough to simply say that humans, too, would do well to "rust" a bit. *Sabi* on iron makes it brittle and useless. But "rusted" humans understand—in an all too human way—the human sentiment; they have an almost primate wisdom. They don't try to exceed their innate limitations.

The word *sabi* offers us a lesson in how we should let things exist as they are.

Utsusemi
Present Body

The prevailing understanding of the word *utsusemi* (*utsushimi*) is that it is the same word as *utsushi-mi* 現し身, which means one's transitory self, one's living body in the real world. But this is misleading.

At the risk of sounding pedantic, I shall explain why it is not that simple. The word *mi* (身) used to have two pronunciations, reflecting two different sources. The *mi* of *utsusemi* was not pronounced in the same way as the *mi* that means one's body (身). So what does that different *mi* mean, then, if not the *mi* of body? The answer is that it's the *mi* (見) of *miru* (見る), which means "to look" or "to see."

The verb *miru* (to look) signifies what human beings experience via sensory perception. The notion that the archaic term *utsusemi* (as 現し, or real embodiment, and 見, to see or perceive via the senses) meant "experiencing something in reality" thus makes sense.

At this point, I should provide a brief explanation of the first half of the term *utsusemi*: *utsuse* (or *utsushi*), which denotes "real embodiment." As the verb *utsutsu* (existing reality) indicates, the word *utsuse* constitutes the very structure that frames reality. But at the same time, the first two syllables of these words— *utsu*—also appear in the verbs *utsusu* 写 and *utsusu* 移, which mean "to copy" and "to relocate," respectively. This may seem a petty point of discussion, but Japanese people have always regarded concrete sensory experience as manifestly real, even if it is only the experience of a duplicate copy or relocated simulation of an unchanging, eternal original Form.

For the premodern Japanese, reality was not merely a perfunctory formality. Just because they performed *misogi* ablutions as a formality did not mean that they could simply leave their sins and impurities of the real world behind and

うつせみ

move on with their lives. The ever-present inner self that remains thoroughly attached to one's person—an essence continually clinging to whatever form we take, as it were—was the *utsusemi*. We moderns really need to rethink what this notion of *utsusemi* means and implies.

In classical prose narratives such as *Genji Monogatari* (*The Tale of Genji*, early eleventh century), we thus often find the word *utsusemi* in a rendering with different characters (*ateji*): the Chinese characters *sora* 空 (sky) + *semi* 蝉 (cicada). Unfortunately, the word *utsusemi* went from meaning a permanent, unchanging reality to denoting something transitory and ephemeral, no doubt due to the influence of Buddhism.

Then again, perhaps this isn't unfortunate. After all, by depicting the world as illusory and temporary, Buddhism gives people the serenity and strength to live. Ultimately, the problem returns to the question of how one can fulfill one's real self.

In our contemporary age, it is particularly hard to achieve a stable sense of self-awareness. Nowhere is it written just what sort of person we are supposed to be or what sort of life we should live.

That makes it all the more necessary that we reconsider the original sense of the word *utsusemi*: one's own real perceptions or experiences. What is important is that we stop living in coerced competition with other people, and instead focus our energies on molding our own everyday experiences into something deeper and more authentic.

My hope is that we might find a way to preserve and treasure this word *utsusemi*—along with the importance of the awareness its nuances entail.

Utakata
■ Foam

The collected works of Mori Ōgai[8]—the preeminent modern author who introduced Western modes to the Meiji literary world—include the story "Utakata no ki" (Foam on the Waves, 1890).

The protagonist of the narrative, set in Germany in the nineteenth century, is a Japanese art student in Berlin who falls in love with a young German girl. Their love comes to a sad, ephemeral end when the girl drowns herself in a lake.

The story depicts a love affair that disappears like froth in water, so *utakata*—the word for bubbles or foam on water, quickly disappearing and amounting to nothing—is a perfectly appropriate title word. In fact, at the time when Ōgai wrote the story, the phrase *utakata no koi* (foam-like love) was already in popular use.

What greatly interests me about the story is that Ōgai used the traditional, distinctly Japanese word *utakata* for the title of a work that would herald a new literary dawn for the Meiji literary establishment and commemorate his experiences abroad in Europe, no less. Later, Ōgai famously described himself as "a conservative progressive." The *utakata* in the title speaks volumes in that regard, crystallizing his unique stance as Western-styled modern literature came to the fore.

The term *utakata* has preserved the type of innate traditional grace that must not be buried under the weight of modernity.

In contrast, the word *hōmatsu*, also meaning "bubbles" or "foam," gives a bad impression. The phrase *hōmatsu kōho* (literally, "foam candidate"), which means something like a joke political candidate who comes to nothing in an election, is a good example. Given those nuances, you can see how thoughtfully and deliberately the Japanese have used *utakata* over time.

Words slowly acquire their beauty over the centuries, through the process of being warmed and polished in the hearts of the people using them.

8. Mori Ōgai (1862–1922)

う
た
か
た

When you mention the word *utakata*, Japanese people immediately recall the opening passage of Kamo no Chōmei's classic essay *Hōjōki* (*An Account of My Hut*, 1212):

The current of the flowing river does not cease, and yet the water is not the same water as before. The foam [*utakata*] that floats on stagnant pools, now vanishing, now forming, never stays the same for long. So, too, it is with the people and dwellings of the world.[9]

The "foam" (*utakata*) that Kamo no Chōmei describes is certainly real: it appears, disappears, and then appears once again, giving it an ever-changing, elusive quality. Almost four centuries later, the great warrior-general Toyotomi Hideyoshi used the term *tsuyu* (dew) in a similar sense in his final death poem:

Tsuyu to ochi	As dew it fell
tsuyu to kienishi	and as dew it vanished—
waga mi kana	my transitory self an empty dream;
Naniwa no koto mo	and what happened in Naniwa
yume no mata yume	was all a dream inside a dream.

One can clearly distinguish the dew (*tsuyu*) of Hideyoshi's poem from "foam." Both denote the same general phenomenon of ephemerality, to be sure. But whereas the phrase "love that disappeared with the dew" (*tsuyu to kieta koi*) expresses the after-effects of love and a sense of vain emptiness, the phrase "froth-like love affair" (*utakata no koi*) expresses the frailty and transience of love itself.

Utakata has occupied a special place in Japanese hearts and minds for centuries, innately evanescent though it may be.

9. See note 8 on page 301

Inishie
◾ Antiquity

The rendering for the word *inishie* (distant past) is a single Chinese character: 古 (old). In classical times, people read *inishie* as *inishihe*.

There is, of course, a more common term that carries the same general meaning: *mukashi* 昔. I have long wondered how these two terms—*mukashi* 昔 and *inishie* 古—differ.

I thought it might have something to do with another word that has the same kind of mysterious structure as *inishihe*: namely, *tokoshihe*. The two words share two common points. First, *ini* is a conjugation of the verb *inu* (去ぬ), which means "to depart" or "to fade away." Morever, *toko* connotes perpetuity, as I explained on page 118. From the fact that both end with *shihe*, however, you can see that these are not your run-of-mill words. The same goes for the word *tamashihi* (the archaic orthography for *tamashii*, the term for "soul"); the *shihi* and *shihe* suffixes carry a certain weight with them.

Another example along the same lines is *sokohi* (depths, abyss). Adding a *hi* suffix to *soko* (bottom) lends the word a deep, mysterious quality. When any syllable from the *ha*-line of the Japanese syllabary appears at the end of a word—as in *inishihe, tokoshihe,* and *tamashihi*—the root word assumes a sense of profound mystery.

In short, you could say that the term *inishihe* exists expressly for the purpose of conveying the times of the distant past, long departed, with a deeper sense of reverence and awe.

いにしえ

By contrast, the term *mukashi* conjures up none of these associations, no sense of mystery. It simply demarcates a clear point in linear time.

The word for "east" is *higashi*. The word for "west" is *nishi*. The word *mukashi* is easy to understand when you orient it with these directional words. These days, we tend to unify time and space into a single conceptual category. The same is true of east and west. Just as east and west simply signify separate directions in a single spatial continuum, the word *mukashi* is simply the past—one direction on the temporal continuum.

At this point, the difference between *mukashi* and *inishihe* becomes plainly clear. *Mukashi* indicates a given temporal point in the past, *inishihe* seems to denote the pinnacle of the mountain of time, the destination of an infinite ascent.

This all ties into the linguistic distinction between *toko* as a notion of eternal time and *toki* as a fixed point in time.

I cannot help but prostrate myself before the depth of *inishihe*, a word with an immeasurable sense of mystery. It is astonishingly easy to comprehend the *mukashi* past—but *inishihe*, with its mystery, reverence, and venerable distant associations, is impossible to know.

The speculative pursuits of past worlds drawn into oblivion—temporal black holes, if you will—do not belong to us moderns alone. The premodern Japanese, as the word *inishihe* suggests, had already embarked on the same quests.

Inishie

いにしえ

Odoki, Medoki

Masculine Time, Feminine Time

P laywright, performer, and dramatic theorist Zeami Motokiyo[10] today occupies the status of the most preeminent figure in the traditional literary and theatrical form called nō drama.

Zeami's masterpiece *Fūshikaden* (Teachings on Style and the Flower, ca. 1402) introduces his ideas on the proper methods for performing nō drama.

In his treatise, Zeami describes how, after decades of working as a nō dramatist and performer, he has come to discern two types of "time" (*jibun*) that a performer experiences on stage. The first type, he argues, refers to the times when the actor's *hana*—his "flower" or, by extension, his "resonating charm"— is in full bloom. The second temporal mode is when his "flower" (*hana*) is not in full bloom. In short, the performer experiences two types of time: those when his powers are vigorous and spirited and those when his physical powers are inactive, subdued. His vitality is always fluctuating: it is never constant or stable.

It is natural that people should always want to perform well. But when the performer thinks purely in terms of the result, or putting on a good show, he tends to push himself too hard. It is precisely this notion of *muri*—of "forcing it"—that Zeami so adamantly rejects. In his view, even a small amount of *muri* will necessarily render the performance an empty and hollow affair, even when the result appears outwardly to have been a success.

Allow me to return to these two types of "time" (*jibun*). The times when the performance naturally goes well, of its own accord, are the times when the actor is brimming with strength and vitality. The other time is when the actor's strength has sunk low, and he finds himself immobile and subdued. With his

---

10. Zeami Motokiyo (ca. 1363–ca. 1443)

strength sapped, the actor must somehow, surreptitiously, figure out a way to channel his latent physical strength. The terms that Zeami gave to these two types of "time" were *odoki* (masculine time) and *medoki* (feminine time).

Zeami then goes on to say that the actor should only take the stage *after* he has fully discerned which type of time he is occupying at that specific moment. Zeami does not indicate that *odoki* "male time" was superior in any way to *medoki* "female time." Rather, he acknowledged the respective essential differences between male and female, and he adamantly insisted that both types of time—*medoki* "feminine" time and the *odoki* virile "masculine" time—each have their own *hana*, their own unique "elegance."

According to Zeami, the awareness of the differences between *medoki* and *odoki* times was the Passing Flower (*jibun no hana*).

That mode of being shows a profound wisdom, an acute awareness of the subtle fluctuations of time. In our daily lives, we all experience these two types of time. There is a time for us to display our "masculine," robust strength; and there is a time for us to show off our "feminine," pliant strength. A time for dynamic movement, and a time for stasis and quietude. There is no mistaking the two: each is beautiful in its own way.

The idea of evenly distributing these two types of time throughout our lives is a concept that all of us would benefit from embracing. Zeami's association of "male" and "female" attributes to time is replete with beautiful, deeply resonant connotations, too.

Wabiru

■ To Deliver a Mortified Apology

W
hen writer Mukōda Kuniko's[11] collection of essays *Chichi no Wabijō* (My Father's Letter of Apology, 1978) met with popular acclaim and the term *wabijō* became something of a buzzword, I couldn't help but think to myself that Japanese people sure love the act of *wabiru*—to apologize.

Apologies bring several things to my mind. Long ago, I said to the late psychologist Kawai Hayao[12] that Japanese say the word *sumimasen* (I'm sorry) as though it's a greeting. "That's right," he immediately said in agreement, and followed with a bad joke: "Even our *sōri daijin* (prime minister) is always quick to say, 'I'm sorry. I'm *sōri*.'"

In the court of law, victims say things like, "I don't want money—what I want is simply that you apologize for what you did!" I suspect this is not always the case, though, in cases of extreme crimes.

What exactly do Japanese people have in mind with this act of *wabi* (apology) that they seem to love so much?

There are two ways to write the word *wabi*: 詫び and 侘び. As far as I can tell, these two Chinese characters are identical in meaning. This is the case both in Japan and China. The word *wabi*, then, is the *wabi* of Sen no Rikyū's[13] *wabicha* tea ceremony. Moreover, *wabi* is a close relative of *sabi*, as in the *wabisabi* concept that Matsuo Bashō took as his ideal in haikai poetry. And *wabi* and *sabi* together both express the lonesome emotional landscape of *wabishii*, a sense of being within close proximity to death. After pondering the subject from various

11. Mukōda Kuniko (1929–1981)   12. Kawai Hayao (1928–2007)   13. Sen no Rikyū (1522–1591)

angles, I came to the conclusion that *wabi* is the emotion one feels when death seems imminent. It was this state of quiet simplicity that both Rikyū and Bashō took as their ideal.

The act of *wabiru* (apology) for one's own errors, then, must imply a deep sense of contrition: to *wabiru* is to make a confession that says, "Having realized my fault, I am now of the mind that I'm essentially as good as dead."

With that in mind, we can well understand the customary phrase, "I will pay with my life" (*shinde o-wabi o shimasu*). The occasional practice of shaving one's head in apology is meaningful precisely because it involves cutting off one's hair—a poignant symbol of one's very own life force—and so it is tantamount to offering an apology by "paying with one's life." In certain nefarious criminal groups, the act of "shortening" your finger in half—*yubi o tsumeru*, as they say— is an indication of *wabi*, of expressing contrition. This, too, is an act of *wabiru* (offering a mortified apology)—by inflicting death upon one small part of one's living being.

But when it comes down it, are we actually cognizant of all this symbolic self-annihilation when we utter these words, "I apologize" (*o-wabi shimasu*)? I doubt it. Simply repeating the word *sumimasen* over and over again in quick succession surely isn't adequate, no matter how many lives one may have. I would like to bring back the moral ideal behind the notion of *wabiru*, invented long ago by the premodern Japanese, who decided that the true meaning of *wabi* (apology) is death.

Ayamaru

To Apologize, To Kill Oneself

In Japanese, the act of apologizing for one's shortcomings or mistakes is expressed by another verb: *ayamaru*. It consists of uttering the word *sumimasen* while bowing your head repeatedly.

What exactly does this act of *ayamaru* (apologizing) involve, though?

From the standpoint of the linguistic principles that form in the evolution of language, we can say that the verb *ayamaru* probably comes from the verb *ayamu*. So what does *ayamu* mean?

Ayamu means "to kill" (*korosu*). In short, the act of apologizing for one's infractions was considered the same as killing someone, believe it or not.

Of course, the victim of that murder is not another person—it is one's own self. The verb *ayamaru* suggests the act of putting oneself in the line of fire, so to speak; of throwing oneself into the deepest depths of the sin committed.

As I mentioned in the essay on *wabiru*, the act of apologizing for one's mistakes, a practice of which we Japanese are so fond, is closely related to the phrase "I will pay with my life."

But if we take just the *aya* part of *ayamaru* and observe it in isolation, we find that the word has an elegant ring. That element probably comes from the fact that *aya* also means *beautiful* in different contexts: expressions like *ayaori* (twill weave) and *me mo aya ni* (beautifully bright eyes).

There are certain similar tropes that will surely be familiar to most: "He shud-

dered in horror at the crime he committed," the narrator might say, "and sought to end his life to make amends." The logic rests on a determination to come clean, to do penance out of contrition. There is even something beautiful in this act of self-annihilation, one might say.

This word *ayamaru* likely came into being in this way, arising out of this departure point of self-determination.

When we reflect on the lurking presence of death behind the word *ayamaru*, we can line up all three acts of apology mentioned before—cutting off one's finger, cropping one's hair, and saying *sumimasen* while bowing one's head in contrition—and see how *ayamaru* has roots in the notion of self-destruction.

Regarding *sumimasen*, no matter how much one apologizes, the word reflects the idea that one's past crimes are so great that one's debts can never be settled. That's why *sumimasen* is a word that requires constant repetition: the gravity of the crime is so great that it can never be paid for. It may sound strange to say, but the verb *sumu* (to finish, to come to an end) connotes the same thing as "to pay." It is only when we have so profusely offered copious apologies—to the point of seemingly paying in full—that a true apology first comes into effect.

Sure enough, *ayamaru* is the most sincere form of apology that a person can give.

Kotowaru
To Decline

W
e often receive requests for favors. Sometimes we are asked to do favors for people.

"Could you pick up something on the way home, honey?"

"Care to join me for dinner tonight?"

We sometimes simply don't feel up to honoring a request, however; at other times, we have prior engagements. We may find it a bit hard, but we have no choice but to say *no* at such times—we all must decline requests and invitations at some point.

This negative response of *no* is expressed in Japanese by the verb *kotowaru*. For things that are a nuisance, too, people put up notices that say "Not taking visitors" (*menkai o-kotowari*), "No solicitation" (*oshiuri o-kotowari*), and "Posting prohibited" (*harigami o-kotowari*).

And yet, incidentally, the original use of the word *kotowaru* was *koto o waru*: to divide things one by one, to classify. It connoted a scrupulous analysis of the inner workings of things.

In other contexts, Japanese people use the word *kotowari* to refer to things pertaining to logic and rationality—as in the "the way of the world" (*yo no kotowari*) and "the ways of men" (*hito no michi no kotowari*), for instance. These are the kinds of things that demand high-level, intellectual judgment, so I was moved the moment I first learned that *koto o waru* implied "reason" and "logical thought." Who knew that the Japanese people—often written off

こ
と
わ
る

as excessively sentimental and ambiguous—could have shown this intellectual capacity for reason?

And so, saying *no*—that is, to *kotowaru*—should imply that one has thoroughly plumbed the depths and comprehended the very heart of the matter at hand in a logical way.

For example, when a recently hired employee asks his boss, "How should we respond to that offer we got?" his supervisor will respond, "Oh, that? Just turn it down flat (*kotowaru*) because it is not worth the trouble!" The scrupulous new employee then responds, "Got it. As you say, it's not worth the hassle. I'll let them know that we will decline (*kotowarimasu*)." Such casual refusals should not be mistaken for *kotowaru* in the original sense of the word.

How lofty and dignified the ethos of the Japanese people who have long regarded the simple act of refusal as tantamount to carrying out reason to its logical conclusion!

Our ancestors also prepared for us that other, emotional verb: *kobamu*—to decline flatly. This term was invented so that we may say *no* with some measure of affect. *Kobamu* expresses a flat-out refusal; there is no need to trouble oneself with logic, as there is with the more intellectually rigorous word *kotowaru*. The example of *kobamu* (flat refusal) that comes to mind is when a woman flatly refuses a marriage proposal from a sleazy guy whom she really dislikes.

Onba-higasa
▪ Pampered Upbringing

In Chinese characters, *onba-higasa* is written *onba* 乳母 (wet nurse) + *higasa* 日傘 (parasol).

Long ago, the native Japanese word *menoto* (wet nurse)—written with the same characters 乳 (breast) and 母 (mother)—referred to the women charged with the task of raising children. Eventually, the word came to be read *uba*. The word *uba*, in turn, came to be called *o-uba*, acquiring the honorific prefix of *o*. *Onba* is simply an accented variation.

The term *onba-higasa*, then, reflects the notion of a child raised in the *onbu ni dakko* style: "carrying your baby on your back and in your arms," literally, or a child wholly dependent on others. The expression is like the English expression "born with a silver spoon in his mouth." In short, *onba-higasa* is the picture of a pampered childhood: a child not only brought up adoringly by a wet nurse (*uba*), who indulges even the slightest desires, but also protected by a parasol to keep his or her skin shielded from the sun.

In the context behind the expression, the wet nurse takes care of the child so dotingly and exhaustively that any observer would reel at the excessiveness of it all and take a jealous and resentful view of the whole situation. However, the term also has a cynical nuance—it views the wet nurse as someone self-sacrificing and blindly obedient—as well as a connotation of pity for the child, one still so weak and immature.

Regardless of what we might think about the *onba-higasa* children we see, we would all surely like to be that spoiled, pampered kid. No matter how many times we disparage those from spoiled upbringings—reviling them because they will "never amount to anything"—most of us regular folk come from households without the luxury of having our own *uba* to look after the children. Only

おんばひがさ

a tiny handful of people are born into such fortunate circumstances.

We cannot deny it: for as much acrimony as we might feel toward pampered kids, it all comes with a twinge of envy, just the same.

When you investigate the specific meaning of the word *onba-higasa*, however, you find that its unique circumstances are virtually unattainable. After all, how many of us are privileged enough to be carried piggy-back in an embrace while having a sun parasol (*higasa*) held over our heads? It's likely that no one has ever actually witnessed such a scene.

Perhaps it is true that no one has even seen this sight. It is precisely this unattainbility that the word seeks to convey. The word is akin to that type of word that expresses something exclusive to the realms of our imaginations. It is analogous, say, to the masses of women who would indulge in fantasies about romance in days of yore, imagining themselves as head over heels in love with handsome, prestigious young men and, accordingly, fool themselves into the belief that those dashing lads might deign to buy them fancy brushes to comb their long, black hair. That fanciful daydream just happens to be the basis of a work song that women planting or hulling rice in the paddies would sing years and years ago.

Put simply, *onba-higasa* suggests some unreal state or unattainable desire. The common folk were determined to overcome their hardships in life by engaging in deliberate self-delusion, by conjuring up fantasies. Aspirational words of hope—the language of yearning—were an expedient tool for that very purpose.

Without this language of escapist reverie, commoners would never have survived their harsh lot. That function of the word *onba-higasa* tears at my heartstrings, I must say.

Teteuchi-hahauchi
Abuse from Both Parents

Japanese has its share of unpleasant words, too, like *teteuchi-hahauchi*: the act of a father (*tete*) and a mother (*haha*) beating (*uchi*) their own child.

That the word is a noun—rather than just a verb—is significant. Had this sort of double parental abuse occurred only once or twice, it would have remained a verb expressing a kind of action. But when the action came to be habitual throughout society and eventually verbalized as a social phenomenon, the noun became a standard way of expressing a common notion.

The increasing frequency with which the noun *teteuchi-hahauchi* appears in the literature shows that, by the eighteenth century, the social phenomenon of abuse from both parents was already rampant in the lowest rungs of Japanese society.

Sad. The word has an oppressive, painful ring to it; it almost hurts just to hear it.

A short aside: I first understood the sorrow of a parent who had lost a child thanks to a small, porcelain "Otsuru" doll at my home when I was a child.

Otsuru is the "pilgrim girl"—the *junrei musume*—who appears in Chikamatsu Hanji's[14] famous *jōruri* puppet play *Keisei-awa no Naruto* (A Courtesan's Ballad of the Crashing Straits of Awa, first performed in 1768). As Otsuru goes from door to door begging for alms for her pilgrimage, she comes upon a certain house. The woman who emerges from that house turns out to be her mother, Oyumi, from whom she had been separated years ago. The mother and daughter don't recognize each other.

Oyumi asks the pilgrim girl, for whom she feels a great deal of pity, about her story. As she inquires into the girl's situation, she starts to ask herself: "Might this girl be my child?" When she eventually asks Otsuru who her father is, the girl answers:

14. Chikamatsu Hanji (1725–1783)

"My father is Jūrōbē."

"And your mother's name?" Oyumi asks.

"My mother is called Oyumi," Otsuru responds.

I can only imagine how Oyumi must have felt. Despite that heartrending revelation, Oyumi is so fearful that some terrible fortune might befall her daughter that she commands Otsuru to return home—and she never reveals her true identity. After leaving, she encounters her father Jūrōbē on the road. Greedily eyeing the money in Otsuru's pocket, he kills her without realizing she is his own daughter.

My mother would always recite that episode from the puppet play to me before the pitiful figure of that Otsuru doll. It was through all those retellings that I learned how heartbreakingly painful the separation between a parent and child could be.

The first instance of *teteuchi* that appears in writing seems to be an episode from the *Kojiki* involving Yamato Takeru, the legendary twelfth emperor of Japan. When his father, Emperor Keikō, instructed his son to go to battle, Takeru responded, "Doth my father command his own son to sacrifice his life?" (*Kojiki*, Book 2). To be sure, much historical time has passed between then and today. But *teteuchi-hahauchi* still happens; its modern incarnations are so horrifying that they defy description. Recent incidents of parents abandoning their own children's corpses are now frequent topics on news programs, and they seem to be becoming a daily occurrence.

If only we could get those monstrous people to understand what their children might be feeling. The word *teteuchi-hahauchi* could prove itself a useful expression: by explicitly verbalizing an unspeakable evil.

Asobu

■ To Play

W hat exactly does this word mean—*asobu*? At its most basic level, the word expresses the state of *bonyari*: that vague, dreamy state of mind. The word's first two syllables—*aso*—are related to *uso*, which means a lie, a deception. (I assure you I am not lying about this.) More fundamentally, *uso* refers to something that lacks substance. There is a related word, *itsuwari*, which denotes something that is "counterfeit" or "false," contradicting real fact.

The vague, indistinct state of *bonyari* was originally a spatial device considered a prerequisite for enabling the divine revelations of the gods to come into one's head. This is why *miko*, shrine maidens who communicate divine commandments, would dance around in circles until they had worked themselves into a frenzy, losing themselves in the dance, and ultimately collapsing to the ground. The accompanying musicians would perform clamorous music that would further push the *miko* to transgress the boundaries of sanity. Accordingly, the act of playing music was expressed with the verb *asobu*.

The divine spirit play known as *kamiasobi* in the Heian period (794–1192) is today called *kagura* 神楽 (sacred music and dance). The reason that the word *asobi* was used for that sort of sacred music, involving inspired movements in the presence of the deities, has a lot to do with the above historical roots.

Now, this act of throwing oneself into a state of *uso*—a state of total emptiness and insubstantiality—eventually came to be performed without the intervention of divine spirits (*kami*). The word *asobi* thus came to express a feeling of auspicious joy and delightful gratification. The human spirit suffocates when the myriad phenomena of this world become too serious, too earnest, and when our energies become focused entirely on practical, day-to-day matters. We start to feel constrained and constricted. Our mood grows totally depressed. Our spirits

become dampened and despondent.

The English word *breakfast* originates in the notion of *breaking* the commandment. It is precisely because one transgresses the law—breaking the injunction not to eat—that a fresh cup of coffee and morning meal taste all the better after fasting.

If it were not for our *asobi* time—this time for transgression, for vacantly tuning out the world—we probably would not even be able to enjoy our breakfast toast and coffee. Imagine a world without this designated time: how dull and restrictive that would be!

A while back, I participated in a TV program alongside several girls who were identified as *hikikomori*, or recluses with social-withdrawal syndrome. When the host of the show told the girls to write down something they liked to do, the girl beside me wrote: "I like giving up." What on earth, I wondered, had thrown this girl into such a bleak and depressive psychological state? The answer, I think, lies in the fact that our modern society rarely gives people the opportunity to throw in the towel, as it were. Simply put: the world doesn't afford people enough chances for *asobi*.

The desire for *asobi* seems stronger in *hikikomori* people than in others. My advice to the girl was simple. "It's all right," I said. "Indulge yourself in a little *asobi* to empty your heart." In this book, too, I would like to encourage any readers who are struggling with similar issues: "Take the time to *asobu*!" Even the steering wheels in cars have a little *asobi*, "play," which is precisely what makes steering the car possible. In short: play makes work possible.

Whisper it in your heart: "I shall *asobu*." It's a vow that will no doubt bring forth a bright landscape before your eyes.

Asobu

あそぶ

Furakoko

■ Hanging Swing

*F*urakoko—a seasonal word classified under spring—is an old word for a hanging swing, or what is today called the *buranko*. In ancient China, it was called the *qiuqian* 鞦韆 (Jp. *shūsen*). At some point, the *furakoko* of old became the *buranko* swing of today. The first parts of the words, *fura* and *bura*, have radically different connotations. *Fura* is elegant and refined, while *bura* has an unclean, vulgar ring on account of its muddied "b" sound. Take, for example, the ugly expression *burabura suru*, which means to wander idly, and compare it to the mellifluous word *furafura*, which expresses the pleasant state of being a bit tipsy. The two expressions are totally different in their connotations. *Burabura* suggests something unsophisticated and in bad taste. Words that start with *fura*—*furakoko* included—are, by contrast, refined and elegant.

If the word *buranko* evokes the sense of a swing dangling loosely there with no one sitting in it, *furakoko* gives the feeling of a swing swaying back and forth in a leisurely, elegant way. I'm fully behind the idea of calling the swing, a ubiquitous playground fixture, by its original name: *furakoko*. There is, of course, another "swing" term that came into use around the tenth century: *yusahari*, derived from the verb *yusaburu*, or "to shake." *Yusahari*, too, seems much better than that ugly word *buranko*.

Playground equipment such as this originated in the northern tribes of China.

People would ride on a leather *qiuqian* around the time of the so-called "cold food" *hanshi* (or Qingming) festival, which fell on the 105th day after the winter solstice. The swing originated sometime in the seventh century BCE in the northern region of China; and when it came down to central China, it became the custom to amuse oneself with it around the start of spring, the so-called *chunjie* 春節 in China or *risshun* 立春 in Japan. Put simply, it was a kind of magical "charm" that people would use at the start of the spring to "swing" everything into movement, injecting a dynamic vitality into the hitherto slumbering, inert mass of wintertime nature.

Therefore, one must not let the *furakoko* dangle inertly in a lackadaisical, *burabura* way—the elegance of *fura* far transcends the disheveled nuances of *bura*. The swing deserves vigor and a grand, swaying motion, a dynamism that sends it flying into the air. The spring sky is flooded with a brilliant radiance, producing a clear, bright serenity. It's enough to make you feel that you might just ascend to heaven and take a seat among the transcendent immortals.

Perhaps this is why Emperor Xuanzong of the High Tang dynasty dubbed the swing, which was hugely popular with his court ladies, the Daoist-sounding name *hansengi*, or "plaything for half-immortals." If you ever take a ride on a *furakoko*, breathe the air deep into your lungs as you dream longingly of spring.

Furakoko

ふらここ

Dorobō-mawari

Taking Turns in Clockwise Order

T he word *dorobō*, which today means "thief," was originally a term in the Kansai dialect that meant a loose liver and a spendthrift. When the word crossed over to the Kantō region, it came to acquire the new meaning of "thief," or *nusubito* in Japanese. Eventually, the word's "thief" denotation went on to achieve complete hegemony over the whole country.

When the word *dorobō*—as thief—gained nationwide currency as a distinct descriptor of a personality type (however appropriate that may be), people also started writing it not only in phonetic *hiragana* but also in Chinese characters: *doro* 泥 (mud) + *bō* 坊 (monk, boy), reflecting the ignominious nature of the word.

At any rate, the nighttime prowler of the *dorobō* made an appearance in several poems in the *Man'yōshū* as *nusubito*. "In the beginning was the *dorobō*," one might say. Evidence of the idea goes back to time immemorial, it seems.

Yet these lawless renegades also had a humorous side from time to time. There were of course many bungling *dorobō*, prone to foolish blunders. Take the famous saying, originally about bumbling thieves: "Hide your head but leave your bum exposed" (*atama kakushite shiri kakusazu*).

The *dorobō* became a kind of pitiable, lovable fellow—so much so, in fact, that *dorobō* characters eventually came to appear in children's games.

Take the practice of a game going around in a circle in *dorobō-mawari* fashion: a clockwise turn. Traditional Japanese kimonos are usually wrapped with the left side over the right; moving in the *dorobō-mawari* pattern, someone on the right could smoothly slide a hand into the pocket of the person to his or her left and, if the player were a thief, pilfer the money in their neighbor's pocket. That way of going around the circle would be advantageous to a *dorobō*, hence the name.

The word *dorobō* always reminds me of the *dorobōgusa*, a type of plant that I learned about when I was a child—the ones with prickly burrs that attach themselves to things and spread their seeds all about. I can remember a time in my garden when a *dorobō-hagi* (*Desmodium* or *nusubito-hagi*) grew so rampant and thick that it became a problem. To be sure, the flower is quite beautiful. The problem is that when you got the slightest bit close to them their seeds stuck right to your clothes and were almost impossible to get off. It's an annoying situation, indeed, made ever worse by the plant's prolific fertility.

Dorobōgusa plants are a true nuisance, yes, but the *dorobō-mawari* turn-taking pattern doesn't mean that the person to your right will reach into your pocket and steal your money. The game just adopts the conniving motion of the *dorobō* to make the game more enjoyable—the *dorobō*'s crime is a light one.

Just a mention of the word *dorobō* is enough to liven up a game. I'd say we could all use a little extra excitement courtesy of the classic thief persona (*dorobō*), one that never fails to entertain us.

Hihina

■ Little One

Since antiquity, the Japanese have had a penchant for using the word *hina* (or its equivalent *hiina*) to refer to small things: *hinadori* (baby chick) in relation to *oyadori* (parent hen), for example, or *hinagata* (miniature model) in contrast to the real thing.

The term *hihina*—which is simply a somewhat elongated pronunciation of *hina*—is often found in a type of fixed verse called *teikeishi*. Poetry—*shiika* 詩歌 in Japanese—has always been an art of rhythm. Naturally, then, lengthening certain phrases and contracting others to align the meter are common techniques. When the word *hina* appears in a poem as its elongated *hihina* (or *hiina*) form, the soft timbre of the *hihina* pronunciation has a sweet, winsome tone. The longer form had such a magnetic pull, in fact, that it established a niche as a word independent from *hina*.

That is the kind of splendid, impressive power that the word possesses.

Allow me to give two examples that illustrate the distinction between *hina* and *hihina*. In company offices, which often resemble war zones, people use the phrase *shōhin no hinagata* to refer to a "product model." The word for little girls playing with dolls, on the other hand, is *hihina asobi*—the extra *hi* fits the essence of the phrase's denotation perfectly.

Because the five sounds of the "*ha*" column of the *kana* syllabary—*ha, hi, hu, he,* and *ho*—are weak and light, a perfectly soft sound emerges when you repeat two of the syllables in a row, such as *haha* or *hihi*. At the same time, the voiced-consonant sound known as *dakuon* (unclear sound) can be an assault on

the ears: the *baba* (the voiced version of *haha*) is the "Old Maid" in the *baba-nuki* card game (the Japanese version of Old Maid); fittingly, the muddled, harsh *dakuon* sounds happen to go with the most dreaded and despised of all the cards in the deck.

Incidentally, the doll-play pastime of *hihina-asobi*, which later evolved into the famous Doll Festival (*hina-matsuri*) in March, originated from an ancient purification ritual. Originally, in the third month of the old lunar calendar, our predecessors would make small doll figurines (*ningyō* 人形, written *hito* or *nin* 人 for "person" + *kata* or *gyō* 形 for "figure")—as stand-ins for use in symbolically casting off impurities and washing away the filth by sending the doll down the river. Ironically, those forsaken, river-bound dolls would one day become the roots of the beautiful *hina-matsuri* dolls (*hina-ningyō*) so dear to many Japanese people's hearts.

A great reversal—from a filthy object to a beloved object—can take place within the Japanese aesthetic consciousness of beauty, which is generally inclined toward small things.

Regardless of what the origins may have been, the word *hina* deserves our affections, as do the *hina ningyō* dolls—but even more than *hina*, the word *hihina* is my expression of choice; the sound is simply more beautifully resonant.

In our contemporary world, things of all kinds are becoming increasingly sloppy and crude. The time is ripe, I think, to reclaim the intricate, delicately tuned sensibility and perception that *hihina* embodies.

Hihina

ひひな

Kaori

■ Scent

*K*aori refers to the smell (*nioi*) that something produces. I've long wondered what the difference was between the two terms *kaori* and *nioi*.
Originally, *kaori* was written with two Chinese characters: *ka* 香 (fragrance) and *ori* 醸 (ferment). *Ka* refers to the vague atmosphere—the *ki* or *qi* 気, which originally meant smell or fragrance—that lingers in the air, *qi* 気 being the imported Chinese term pronounced as either *ki* or *ke* in Japanese.

The second character, *ori* 醸, denotes the process by which *sake* gradually ferments, acquiring its rich, mellow flavor. The premodern Japanese presumably used *kaori* for anything that had a rich aroma that would waft through the air.

This must be why the greatest compliment you can give a person regarding their personality is to say that their singular "*kaori*" comes across clearly.

Nioi (originally written *nihohi*), on the other hand, used to refer to the red color known as *ni* or *ni-iro*, which originally signified the red earth tones that materialize in the ground: *ni* becoming 秀 (*ho*), or conspicuous.

Accordingly, the word *nioi* originally expressed the process of a color becoming conspicuous but eventually came to be used for anything that wafts in. When *ka* (fragrance) manifests itself, it becomes a *nioi*. As a result, *nioi* came to resemble *kaori*.

The Chinese character for *nioi*—匂—is a *kokuji* (国字), or "national Chinese

かおり

characters" native not to China but rather to Japan. The character resembles the Chinese character 匀, which originally meant "echo" or "reverberation" (*hibiki*). The made-in-Japan Chinese character captures the rather splendid interpretative conceit of the premodern Japanese, who apparently conceived *nioi* as a special resonance.

The word *jinkaku* (personality or character) indicates the tone (*neiro*) that resonates within a person. This notion of sound-as-character comes from the West; the word's circumstances abroad are equivalent in Japan. Moreover, the word *nioi* suggests that our forebears grasped the concept of "personality" as the tantalizing sparkle—or *hanayagi*—that *jinkaku* evokes. I find this, too, a wonderful insight. The wafting, atmospheric quality (*tadayoi*) of a person's natural demeanor, the tantalizing gleam that emerges from their personality—although the specific denotations may differ, their wonders match in perfect unison. I often come across explanations that people should use the word *kaori* for a pleasant smell and the word *nioi* for a bad one, but that would be too reductionist: the matter is far more complex and defies such arbitrary solutions.

Happily enough, *kaori* has maintained a purely unchanging heart, unlike the word *nioi*, whose meaning has changed considerably over the centuries.

Kaori

———

かおり

Hanada
Light Blue

T
he word *hanada* 縹 is exclusively used as a color descriptor, specifically related to the color blue, which is *ao* 青 in Japanese. The fact that *hanada* refers to a shade of blue might come as a surprise to some.

The word *hanada-iro* (*iro* meaning "color") is often abbreviated as *hanairo*. Most Japanese people are familiar with the phrase "the lining in *hanairo* cotton" in reference to a chic kind of kimono. I must confess that for a long time, I also assumed that *hanairo* lining material was a bright red color or some similar hue. But my assumption was dead wrong: it was blue lining, to my astonishment.

There's also a type of charming little autumn plant called the *tsuyukusa*, literally "dew grass," whose English name is the Asiatic dayflower. Given its blue flowers, the plant also goes by the name *hanadagusa*—*hanada* (light blue) + *gusa* (grass).

At this point, you're probably wondering how it came to be that a shade of blue acquired the *hanada* alias. I'm sorry to say that I don't know the answer. Perhaps it originated in an ancient custom from the Heian period (794–1192), when people would use the term *hanada* to describe the fashion of wearing doubled layers of overlapping blue on blue. I'd like to think that, seeing as how the history of the word is so long, the premodern Japanese regarded blue as the highest pinnacle of suave elegance and refinement.

The blue color that we call *ao* (青) has long been regarded as neither light nor dark, but rather some indefinable middle. Our forebears were insightful enough

to associate the ultimate in beauty with a color in that nebulous secondary stratum, seeing a comparatively muted color as more elegant than a bold counterpart. Knowing that people around a millennium ago had those sensibilities delights me. They applied the same logic to red: to them, red that was simply vivid, unadulterated brightness *sans* darkness was too unrefined, too simple.

Is that sophistication not a mark of a high-level civilization? From now on, I'd like to stop referring to blue with the word *ao* (blue); *hanada-iro* is much more suitable, in my eyes.

The eminent modern poet Nakahara Chūya,[15] who lived a tragically short life, also loved the color *hanada* and the connotations it evoked. In his renowned poem "Asa no uta" (Morning Song, 1928), for example, we find the following two lines:

> Kotorira no uta wa kikoezu　　I cannot hear the little bird's songs
> sora wa kyō hanadairo rashi.　　The sky today seems light blue [*hanada-iro*].

The common name *tsuyukusa*—dayflower, dew-grass—is no doubt beautiful, but so is the name *hanadagusa*. The character for *hanada* (縹), too, has a beautiful appearance. Given the word's alluring charm, there has to be some chic bistro around here with the name "Hanada."

15. Nakahara Chūya (1907–1937)

Hanada

はなだ

Tatsu

■ To Stand Forth

*T*atsu is a word that we use so regularly in our daily lives that it's as familiar to us as a cup of tea. But what does it word mean, exactly? When someone says *tachinasai!*—which generally means "stand up"—for instance, what is the correct thing to do?

The problem, you see, takes on new layers when you realize that common *tatsu* expressions like *chōshū ga doyomekitatta* (the audience stirred; *tatta* is the past-tense form of *tatsu*), *kare wa sakkidatta* (he grew menacing; *datta* is also the past-tense form of *tatsu* in some phrasings), *hara ga tatte shikata nai* (I was angry beyond toleration; *tatte* is another form of *tatsu*), and *omokage ni tachikuru kojin* (the dead appearing in an apparition; *tachikuru* contains the same Chinese character as *tatsu*), to name a few, contain no elements suggestive of the act of "standing up."

In the first two compound verb cases—*doyomekitatsu* and *sakkidatsu*—tacking on the verbal suffix *–tatsu* adds a certain force or momentum to the root verb. *Doyomekitatsu* seems to suggest that people's moods somehow resound and make a stir in a gathering of momentum and force. *Sakkidatsu*, meanwhile, connotes a kind of agitation with an almost murderous intensity, a product of tremendous momentum and force.

The third expression—*hara ga tatsu* (to become angry)—suggests a condition where one's emotional "stomach" is left wanting, unsoothed, and therefore seethes with anger. Thus, one can claim with certainty that the word *hara* (stomach) originally meant *kokoro* (feelings or heart). A heart (*kokoro*) brimming with indignation is akin, then, to a "stomach" (*hara*) jerking upright (*tatsu*). This sense of the verb *tatsu* denotes the process by which something calm and at rest suddenly rouses and becomes a vigorous force.

In that light, the fourth phrase—*omokage ni tatsu* (the visage of the dead appearing before one's eyes)—suddenly makes sense, as well. Here we see the same process at work: something that had quietly and calmly concealed itself suddenly assumes a vitality and concrete form.

In this case, then, writing *tatsu* as 顕つ with the Chinese character 顕—which means "to become manifest"—is certainly more appropriate than writing it with the usual character 立, which simply means "to stand." I have already explained elsewhere how *aru* (在る) *koto* and *aru* (生る) *koto* share the same essential meaning[16]; the *aru* pair was born from this same notion of an entity gaining momentum and vigor, thereby bringing it into existence.

We may say that the Japanese verb *tatsu* is closest to the Chinese character 顕, meaning to move from latent potential to manifest presence. Before a thing appears (*tatsu*), it is invisible to the eye. It is through this process of becoming manifest (*tatsu*) that a thing discloses itself and becomes present (*arawareru*). As I noted above, the *ara* of *arawareru* carries the same meaning as *aru* 生る (to live or exist). The word *tatsu* thus undoubtedly came into existence on the premise of things existing.

I would like you to keep this fact in mind the next time someone tells you to stand up: *o-tachi kudasai!* Unless you commit to assuming your true, vigorous appearance and stand up to full height in a stately manner, your head high with the zest of youth, it won't truly qualify as *tatsu* in the original sense of the word.

And when your little one is commanded to "stand" (*tachinasai*) by his kindergarten principal, you, as his knowledgeable parent, must be sure to tell him to "stand up, carry yourself proudly, and look alive!"

---

16. See page 194

Tatsu

たつ

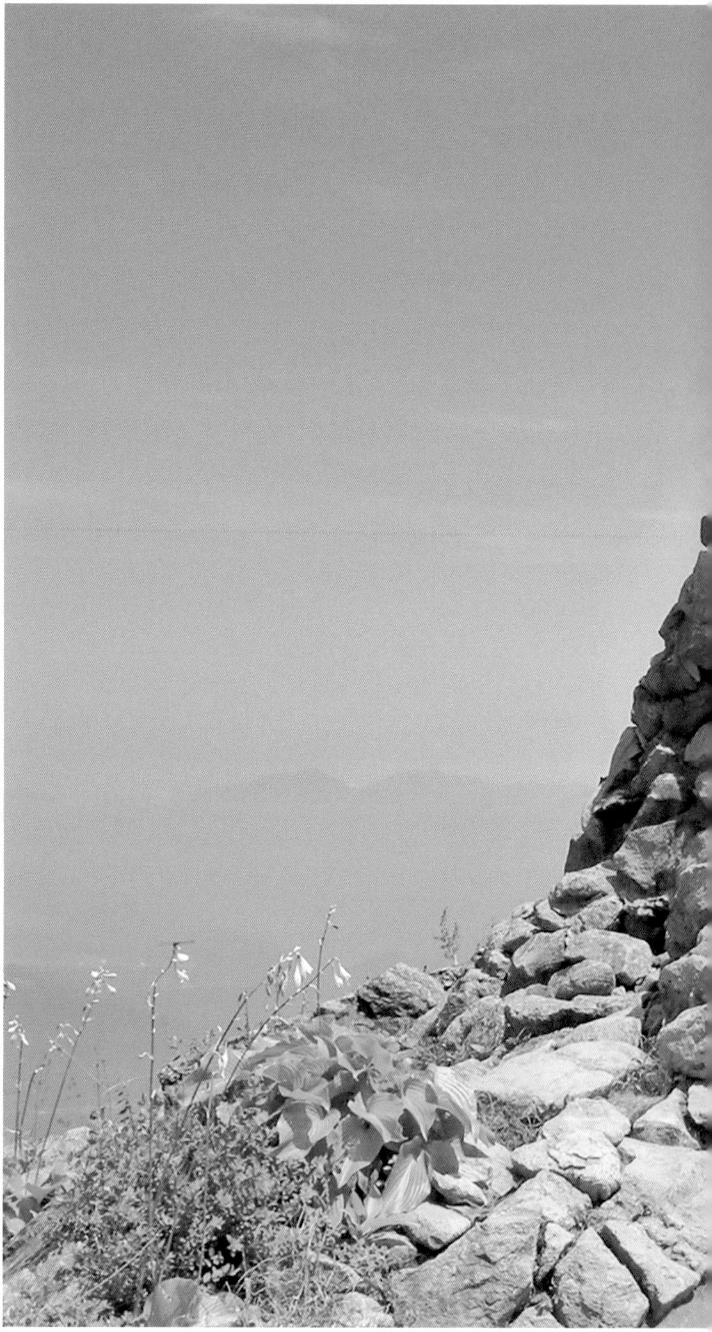

Tebon

■ Passing a Bowl without a Tray

W hen I first encountered the word *tebon* 手盆 many moons ago, I couldn't understand its meaning. *Te* 手 (hand) and *bon* 盆 (tray)? A "hand tray?" When it finally occurred to me what it meant, though, I was so astonished that I nearly jumped with joy. "I can't believe such a word actually exists!" I exclaimed to myself.

The word has roots in tradition, particularly meal etiquette. For example, when a guest would hand over an empty *chawan* (bowl) to get a second helping of something, the server would normally hold out an *o-bon* (tray) for the guest's bowl to go on; it was rude for servers to take empty bowls and give them back to guests by hand. But what if there was no *o-bon* around? If servers had no other choice but to receive and return *chawan* with their hands, however, they would say, "*Tebon de shitsurei shimasu.*" In English: "Please forgive me for using my *tebon* (hand tray)."

The "tray" custom went beyond traditional bowl manners. Long ago, people practiced the custom with a wide assortment of items, placing them on actual trays or *sensu* (Japanese fans) for proper handling. Presenters at awards ceremonies are supposed to offer the certificates only *after* they've placed them on an *o-bon* tray for proper offering to the recipient. But nowadays, people no longer take the time to do such elegant things. Worse yet, people aren't even aware that it is considered rude not to do so.

The next time you're about to hand something over to someone, then, how about putting it on a tray? It's worth a thought.

Think about what it means to liken the *te* (hand) to the *bon* (tray) to make up for a lack of a proper tray. The word *tebon* strikes me as the height of superb refinement, graceful modesty, and cultivated restraint. We modern folk have lost the ability to think in terms of *mitate*—literally, "seeing by comparison"—or figuratively finding parallels in the dissimilar. At the very least, I want people to prepare a metaphorical "tray," using their hands in a *mitate* fashion, on those necessary occasions.

The same can be said about the word *karacha*—"tea without cakes"—which is written with two characters: "empty" (*kara* 空) and "tea" (*cha* 茶). When a host has no cakes or sweets to offer a guest with tea, he or she should say, with a twinge of apology, "*Karacha desu ga*" ("Here is a cup of tea, without cakes, I'm afraid"), and then proceed to serve the tea without its usual accompaniment. One should never blurt, "Sorry, but I don't have any cakes or sweets for you!" The same goes for the *o-bon* tray; one cannot just announce gruffly, "Sorry, but there's no tray!" (*bon wa nai yo*). It was to avoid such curt inelegance that the medieval Japanese people came up with the notion of *karacha*, just as they had come up with the phrase *tebon* for avoiding having to say, "There's no tray."

Words possess a more than adequate ability to compensate for the impropriety that can come with mere material insufficiency. That's a power we should all take to heart.

Anza

- Sitting with One's Legs Crossed

Most people know about the formal method of sitting called *seiza*, which literally means "proper sitting." *Seiza* is said to have originated as a form of punishment. Seeing how unbearably unnatural and uncomfortable the *seiza* style is, I find myself easily convinced by that explanation.

The "proper style" of *seiza* sitting seems to have first come into practice during the feudal era of *buke* (samurai rule), which lasted from the early thirteenth to the late sixteenth century. If you look at earlier paintings from the Nara (710–794) and Heian (794–1192) periods, you find that the emperor and his high-ranking ministers would always sit with their legs folded in a leisurely, relaxed position. But by the time cross-legged sitting came to be known formally as *agura* (胡 trouble, reckless + 坐 sitting), the feudal military government officials had already started to seek out a more austere and formal way of sitting. What they came up with was the "correct" or "proper" method of *seiza*.

The old style of relaxed, cross-legged sitting preceded *seiza*, then. That less formal manner eventually came to be called *anza*, written with the two Chinese characters: *an* 安 (easy and relaxed) + *za* 座 (sitting). This reminds me of those people who start to call a normal, non-express train "the slow train" as soon as a high-speed express train starts to serve their neighborhood.

The *anza* style also happens to have been extremely comfortable. Indeed, its appearance seemed to signal that our modes of sitting had at least regained a certain degree of humaneness.

Even though the relaxed *anza* style preceded formal *seiza*, whenever I find myself at someone's house, I always start by unconsciously assuming the *seiza* posture. After some time, when I am invited to switch to the more comfortable

anza style, I find that the cramped stiffness and tension in my mind and body suddenly come undone; the release invigorates my mind and body; I feel a certain sense of liberation.

The word *anza* itself—*an* 安 (easy and relaxed) + *za* 座 (sitting)—evokes that sense of liberation, as though the word alone has the power to release us from the tensions of this corporeal world. Sitting in *anza* simply makes us feel good. Whenever you're about to sit cross-legged and relaxed, I ask that you refer to it not in the usual way as "*agura o kaku*" (cross-legged style) but rather say, "*Anza o itashimasu!*": "I shall now sit in a relaxed pose!"

It's worth noting, too, that the figures of *hotokesama*—enlightened Buddhas—in Buddhist iconography are always sitting in this relaxed *anza* position. The austere, meditative practice called *zazen*—literally, "Zen sitting," 座 (sitting) + 禅 (Zen)—is also originally a form of *anza*. When you sit that way, you feel none of the pain or discomfort that more formal postures, such as *seiza*, invariably bring. The *anza* (and *zazen*) posture can fortify your inner spirit into a single unified whole, clearing your mind in the process.

I can't even imagine drinking *sake* in any other position than the relaxed *anza* style. The only time people imbibe sitting in the formal *seiza* style is when they perform the so-called *sansankudo,* or "thrice three, nine times" ceremonial exchange of nuptial cups, or when they drink the spiced medicinal *sake* called *o-toso* traditionally served during New Year celebrations.

Don't be bothered by the almost foreign-sounding ring of *anza*, a word that sounds like it must have originated in a language like Sanskrit or Chinese. I dare say the word's exotic ring is what makes it even more enchanting.

Kazashi

■ Traditional Hair Ornament

The term *kazashi* survives in contemporary Japanese in an associated form, *kanzashi*.

Originally, a *kazashi*—an ornamental hair pin—was called a *kami-sashi*, which refers to the act of inserting an object into one's hair or, alternately, the object itself. The *n* of *kanzashi* is a rustic variation of the *mi* in *kamisashi*.

The original *kazashi* were plants, commonly ears of rice (*inaho*). That tradition of rice-ear hair adornment lives on today, remarkably, in the traditional Japanese hairstyle known as *Nihongami*. In the classic rice-ear motif, you can make out what the premodern Japanese were doing by putting plants in their hair: aiming to receive the plant's essential "spirit"—what we call *ekisu* (extract) in modern Japanese.

Nowadays, people enjoy steeping themselves in the vapors of trees, calling the practice "forest bathing." *Kazashi* was a more direct, more concrete version of that same thing: receiving a plant's essential spirit through the medium of their hair.

This doesn't simply mean, though, that you can just slip any old plant into any old place on your body to extract a powerful essence. The *kazashi* tradition ties into a biological phenomenon: the fact that our hair and fingernails continue to grow throughout our entire lives. Our vitality is so vibrant in our hair, for example, that the life force refuses to expire—and that makes it the proper place for the extracts of plant energy to flow in.

Until recently, people saw *kazashi* as a kind of charm, a brand of "contagious magic." For all practical purposes, though, they meant to become infected by the plant's *ekisu*, which they regarded as a kind of contagious element. The practice deserves a reputation as a technique for a contagious means of wellbeing rather than a form of witchcraft.

The premodern Japanese were especially earnest in their belief that human beings and nature are indivisibly linked. They believed, moreover, that each individual human was connected to a specific individual tree. Indeed, the field of anthropology has recently produced various reports about how our predecessors regarded each tree to be an index of a specific human life. The *kazashi* custom is not limited to a particular tree, but it clearly stems from the values of humans dwelling in deep connection with the natural world.

And yet, when the materials for *kazashi* switched from plants to metals, people could no longer expect the essence inhabiting plants to seep into their beings. Instead of simply substituting plants for metals, we would do well to decorate our lapels with a few flowers that we happen to find on the side of the road. That would be so much more fulfilling, so much more spiritually enriching, than using a crude, lifeless metal object.

The word *kanzashi* is far from refined or beautiful in its sound—in fact, it has a rather rustic ring to it. Perhaps we would be better off reverting the term to the antiquated *kazashi*, a return of the heart to a flourishing essence.

Kazashi

かざし

Katsura

Hairpiece

Today, the term *katsura* survives only in two senses: as the name for the tree known as the *katsura* (桂) and the word for "wig" (鬘). Originally, the term denoted a type of hair ornament, made from a plant, called the *kamitsura* 髪連—the characters for "hair" and "connect"—which was used to wind around a person's head.

Like the *kazashi* hair ornament (the previous essay), *katsura* were believed to make it possible for the tree's "life extract"—what we call *ekisu* in Japanese—to seep into a person's hair. Originally, however, *katsura* began when our ancestors discovered that wrapping plants around one's head (*kamitsura*) has certain physical functions, much like the supposed functions of the Japanese *hachimaki* or those bandanas you find abroad. It was said that one could stimulate the workings of your brain by wrapping the *katsura* in your hair. Eventually, the *katsura* became a decorative embellishment, reaching the point where people would put an assortment of hawk feathers into it like some great village chief.

The *katsura* phenomenon began in classical Japan in the form of winding a crown of vines on one's head. Vines such as the *hikage no kazura*—literally, "sunlight vine," or club moss—were also among the plants that people believed would act as a surrogate in place of the sun's radiance.

The *katsura* headpieces of ancient Greece were, in contrast, made with olive leaves. They were thought to be bestowed from the god Apollo. In ancient

かつら

Greece, olive crowns (or laurel crowns) were accolades for victors in war. In Japan, however, female *miko* spiritual mediums wore "sunlight vines" (*hikage no katsura*) and offered their dances to the gods.

The *katsura* hairpieces that remained in use, with their concomitant beliefs intact, were the *katsura* made from the willow tree (*yanagi*) in China and Japan. In China, there is an ancient melodic poem titled "Breaking the Willow Tree," which was performed at farewell occasions for friends.

I suppose that the attendees at farewell parties would make each other *katsura* wreaths of willow branches and then offer prayers for one another's long life, happiness, prosperity, and so forth. Willow trees have an especially short life span but also exhibit an astoundingly prodigious vitality, a nature that led the premoderns to attach substantial value to the species.

It is greatly regrettable that today the *katsura* has completely lost its original essence. Artificial hairpieces and wigs are no doubt important, but I can't help but doubt that we will ever see women reviving the *katsura* custom and winding plants into their hair.

The *katsura* phenomenon is always striking to me in its depth. Even a single willow branch given as a farewell gift has the power to convey a sense of respect for the ancient custom of willow-tree *katsura*. It is precisely at such moments that the long, curiously intriguing history of the *katsura* comes back to life.

Katsura

かつら

O-sagari
Hand-Me-Downs

Honestly, I was shocked when I first learned that the word *o-sagari*—literally, "something passed down"—originally meant a gift from a deity. Until then, you see, I had thought that the word simply referred to those old articles of clothing that get passed down to you from your older siblings. Friends of mine often make the same mistake. "This is just a hand-me-down from my older brother," they blush.

In antiquity, imperial gifts were called *roku* 禄, a word that generally means "beneficent gifts," usually in the form of clothing. As the radical 衤 in Chinese characters suggests, these "divinely bestowed" gifts generally consisted of clothing; occasionally, though, they came in the form of money or other items. There is, of course, the "precious imperial gift of clothing" (*onshi no gyoi*) that Sugawara no Michizane[17] famously received. Also, what we now call a "seasonal bonus" (extra pay) used to be called *kiroku* 季禄, or "seasonal *roku*": clothing and kimono robes bestowed according to the season. One's annual salary, too, used to be called *hōroku* 俸禄, which also came in the form of clothing and kimono robes.

It's no wonder, then, that *o-sagari* hand-me-downs did indeed involve used clothing; only rarely did it involve other items.

When my father passed away thirty-four years ago, I received an *o-sagari* coat from him. For the first few years, I wore it from time to time. Even today, I still hold my *o-sagari* dear.

I was delightfully surprised and moved when I learned that rains that fall on

---

17. Sugawara no Michizane (845–903)

おさがり

New Year's Day are also called *o-sagari*. Naturally, everyone hopes and prays for clear skies on the auspicious occasion of New Year's Day—but it's certainly not the case that clear skies are necessarily better. Deities (*kami*) sometimes bestow merciful rains, or *jiu* 慈雨, on New Year's Day. As a matter of fact, spring sets into motion with each rainfall. Rain is no doubt a necessary gift that helps bring an end to the dried-up, withered winter. If this isn't a quintessential example of the god-bestowed gifts of *o-sagari*, I don't know what is.

Now that I have mentioned my father, I might as well be so bold as to include his final poem, which he wrote on his deathbed and bequeathed to me along with the other *o-sagari*, his coat:

O-sagari ya	Hand-me downs!
shizuka ni tomoru	God-bestowed lights
kami no shoku	flickering quietly

Every meal is a gift from the gods—an *o-sagari* of sustenance. That is the idea behind the custom of saying *itadakimasu,* too—the phrase expresses receiving nourishment with a humble heart—before we begin eating.

Nevertheless, I recently heard that a certain school has stopped requiring its pupils to say *itadakimasu* at lunchtime. Apparently, the PTA filed a complaint contending that the children aren't being "bestowed" anything by the teachers, so the *itadakimasu* custom shouldn't apply. What is this world coming to?

Sugatami
Full-Length Mirror

"*Sugata ga ii*"—which means something like "My, what a nice appearance you have!"—is one of those compliments that people don't throw around lightly.

The word *sugata* (figure, form) here doesn't simply mean one's build or physical appearance, of course. It also refers to the "form" of one's day-to-day mode of living, one's poise in handling practical matters, one's comportment in action.

Sugata thus has two dimensions: the external *and* the internal. You might think of the phrase *mi no konashi*—one's carriage, movement, or bearing—as the resplendent movements of a *sugata*.

In that same vein, *sugatami*—written with the two Chinese characters *sugata* (figure) and *mi* 見 (to look)—is a large, full-length mirror that reflects your *sugata* in its entirety. It's a kind of magical *ōkagami*, or "great mirror," that reveals every facet of your self, all the way down to your psychological disposition and the way you carry yourself. The last syllable of *sugatami*—*mi* 見—is the same *mi* as the *mi* of *miru* 見る, meaning "to see" or "to look." But in the context of this word *sugatami*, *mi* suggests not only "to see" but also "to praise" or "to admire."

So, why is it that we tend to feel anxious and uneasy about seeing ourselves in

a *sugatami* full-length mirror? What is it about our reflected selves that make us feel so dejected, so disheartened? Why do we perceive ourselves as so worn out, so exhausted, so lackluster?

That's why the *sugatami* is so vital—the mirror reflects psychological interiority *and* physical exteriority, giving us a barometer for our everyday selves. Among the words in vogue during the Edo period (1603–1868) was the word *sugata-sakari*, which means something like "one's *sugata* in top form." No matter how many years we put on or how forlorn and dejected we might feel, we all want to see ourselves in our *sugata-sakari*, our peak shape, whenever we look into the mirror.

I have long suspected that the etymological origin of the word *sugata* can be traced to two words: *su* 衣 (clothing) and *kata* 形 (form). The premodern Japanese believed that dressing well and possessing a dignified inner disposition go hand in hand. Of course, just because someone owns expensive clothes doesn't mean they have an honorable character.

When one's inner disposition and external appearance show themselves in perfect unison—this is the very definition of an appealing *sugata*.

Kusamakura

A Pillow of Grass

Kusamakura, or "grass pillow," refers to the act of sleeping outside in the open air on a "pillow" of grass—the meaning is self-evident.

Surprisingly few people know, however, that the term is also a metaphor for a journey, or *tabi* in Japanese, and occupies a semantic space between *tamakura* (literally, "arm pillow") and *iwamakura* (literally, "rock pillow").

Tabi is the opposite of *ie*, the word for "home." That is, the two words are antonyms. If a journey (*tabi*) finds its symbolization in the image of the *kusamakura*, where does the home (*ie*) locate its pillow analogy? The answer is *tamakura*, an "arm pillow."

In short, our ancestors held the view that the home is a safe, peaceful dwelling where one lives a quiet, domestic life. Once you leave that home and embark on a journey, wandering through the wild, you have no choice but to look for grass as a pillow. In point of fact, the people of antiquity used to cut plants such as the sedge and make them into pillows.

The origins of the word *makura* (pillow) lie in *maku*, the verb that means "to wrap." Accordingly, the idea of the *makura* began in the image of a lover's arm, wrapping itself around the sleeper. After all, the home is where one can take solace in the embrace of a loved one's arms: the place with a *tamakura*. On the proverbial road, the only replacement for that warm arm is grass, a crude, natural substitute. The "pillow" one uses on a journey is the *kusamakura*; the metaphors align.

Incidentally, a person who died on the road during an arduous journey would be laid to rest on the roadside surrounded by rocks, or *iwa*. When we place this notion beside *tamakura* and *kusamakura*, we might call it *iwamakura*, or "rock pillow."

Therefore, *kusamakura* evokes the sense of grief that comes with missing a loved one. When the young Prince Arima no Miko[18] was banished from the capital after being framed for a crime, he composed a rather moving poem that was later included in Book 2 of the *Man'yōshū*. To paraphrase: "When at home, I ate my meals served on a plate; but now that I am on a *kusamakura* journey, I serve myself food on the leaves of trees." Note the superb contrast between home (*ie*) and journey (*tabi*). To paraphrase this poem in terms of *tamakura* (arm pillow): "On this lonesome journey, devoid of my beloved *tamakura*, lacking even the most basic plates and utensils, I pile food on leaves to eat in solitude." For a long time thereafter, the role and joy of wives has been to serve food to their husbands at home, on plates. The importance of this word *kusamakura*—grass pillow—lies paradoxically in that it conveys a lack of *tamakura*: its emotional appeal resonates the absence of love. Likewise, homes that had lost their beloved wives—and by extension their beloved *tamakura* arm pillows—caused our ancestors tremendous grief.

It would be a tremendous cultural loss if we were to forget this word *kusamakura*, not only because it presents a metaphor for the lonesome journey but also because it conjures up a longing for the comforting haven of the home.

---

18. Arima no Miko (640–658)

Essays on Modes of Living

"To Acquire One Thing is to Lose Another"

Contemporary author Kuroi Senji[1] is a virtuoso of language. Quite a few writers scribble away without economy or concision. Kuroi Senji, however, brings his ideas together into concise unity through precise expression.

In his collection of essays called *Oi no Tsubuyaki* (Mutterings of an Old Man, 2012), for example, he refers to the recent fad of worshipping youth as "an ersatz attempt at rejuvenation" (*misekake no wakagaeri*). He also describes the black and white stones used in the traditional Japanese strategy board game called Go as "nameless stones, all perfectly equal, without any official title."

Kuroi is supremely adept at bringing out the subtleties of language.

His collection of essays brims with astonishing statements and phrases that make the reader's heart skip a beat. One of his most striking claims is that "to acquire one thing is to lose another" (*hitotsu o eru koto wa hitotsu o ushinau koto demo aru*).

How many people in our world these days can grasp the significance of this statement? Don't most people simply judge things according to whether they might increase one's possessions? Very few, if any, would agree with the seemingly radical statement that addition and subtraction occur simultaneously.

After all, everyone knows that one plus one makes two, not one. Kuroi, however, maintains that one plus one makes one. It's strange, right?

But when you stop to consider his remark at a deeper, more essential level, his point becomes crystal clear. Everything in the universe is part of a single, uniform, finite, whole substance. The idea of adding something without an equal something being subtracted is thus logically impossible. For instance, when your savings increase by an amount of, say, one yen, the amount of money in someone else's account necessarily diminishes by one yen. It's a notion central to the popular Japanese expression, "Money will come and go, never staying long in the

1. Kuroi Senji (b. 1932)

same hands" (*kane wa tenka no mawari mono*).

Most people, however, only have eyes for profit. When they find that funds on hand have disappeared, they often endeavor to acquire money no matter what the means. When they can't make up for their loss, they'll curse their fate.

Kuroi's notion that acquiring one thing necessarily implies the loss of another effectively throws a bucket of cold water onto "worldly" common sense. It also serves as a key to unlocking the secret of happiness.

Come to think of it, the late businessman Hiraiwa Gaishi[2] once said something that strikes a similar chord. "To emerge victorious," he said, "one only has to win only by a margin of 60%." What this statement means is that we should be willing to sacrifice 40%.

In other words, we shouldn't let greed take hold and commandeer our minds toward total victory. Hiraiwa warns us that we only incur resentment when we aim for complete triumph. The best thing would be to finish our battles in a split draw, I suppose. Yet given that the word *shōbu* 勝負—competition—includes the characters for both "win" (勝) and "lose" (負), competing means you must do one or the other. It's obviously better to win, in that case. And when we do come out on top, the ideal margin of victory is right around 60%—a win by the score of 6 to 4, say. In effect, it's about one win and one loss every time; to "win" one is to "lose" another.

---

2. Hiraiwa Gaishi (1914-2007)

"Accumulate Virtue!"

There is a certain mysterious, poignant quality that runs through much of contemporary Japanese painting. For a long time, I struggled to put my finger on it, something that makes us question the true essence of things—and something you won't find in mediocre works.

I recently found a linguistic rendering of that ineffable quality: *shin'in hyōbyō* 神韻縹渺, a critical term for a work of art that is "sublime" or "transcendent." The term consists of two words: *shin'in* 神韻 (divine sound) and *hyōbyō* 縹渺 (faint and ephemeral).

I'd even venture to say that this is a common thread uniting virtually all pictorial beauty, resonating through all masterpieces.

To be sure, the sense of authenticity that emanates from masterpieces stems from their ability to go beyond mere representation, beyond mere portrayals of actual form. Instead, what emerges from these canvases is a fragrance of the very divine, mystic air itself.

That's the prize for which artists strive so hard; they agonize over how to convey that transcendent tone of *shin'in* (divine sound) in their paintings.

Mulling over the concept of *shin'in hyōbyō*, I recalled something artist Tezuka Yūji (b. 1953) once said. Tezuka is an outstanding painter who outshines many of the older painters who dominate the world of Nihonga, a genre of modern Japanese painting. For instance, in his acclaimed painting "Tsukuyomi" (Moon God), the entire surface of his canvas appears to glow in a clear moonlight—the work is a true masterpiece that resonates with the serene, tranquil heartbeat of the ocean's vast mystery.

Tezuka once said that celebrated Nihonga painter Hirayama Ikuo[3] offered him some advice about how to be a great painter. The advice consisted of a simple command: "Accumulate virtue!" (*Toku o tsume!*).

"Hirayama-sensei hardly ever spoke," Tezuka explained. "He would simply

---

3. Hirayama Ikuo (1930–2009)

repeat these words: 'Accumulate virtue!'"

What I read took my breath away.

For at that moment, something astonishing suddenly occurred to me. His remark made me finally realize the true meaning of that expression *shin'in hyōbyō*: the austere and virtuous spirit of the artist permeating the canvas.

Tezuka did not elaborate, of course. He simply passed down the advice that his teacher, Master Hirayama, had imparted to him. After all, the personification of *shin'in* itself lies beyond the realm of explanation.

The paintings of Hirayama—who so wisely advised the next generation of painters—convey a richly lingering sense of *shin'in*, encompassing the figures and objects depicted therein. I once had the opportunity to exchange views with several noted scholars about Hirayama's paintings. To my surprise, most of them often used the word "fantastical" (*gensōteki*) to describe his work. I'd beg to differ. I've always felt that the blurry outlines of objects, figures, and landscapes in his paintings, though seemingly "fantastical" on the surface, actually represent the true essence of things—the *mono no hontai*, as we say. His work captures a deeper reality that resonates forth when one has thoroughly probed the nature of things—and in order to absorb that broader structure of reality, one must first accumulate human virtues, or *jintoku* 人徳.

The Chinese character *toku* 徳 originally referred to a mind or heart (*kokoro*) with a "direct and upright" (*massugu*) quality, a sense of forthright sincerity. A clear, knowing state of mind—not concerned with the banal matters of depicting the world skillfully or aiming to produce a masterpiece—is what gives the art the quality of *shin'in*.

Virtue is what leads us to strive for loftier heights and to realize our authentic selves.

There is a well-known passage from the *Analects of Confucius* that says, "Virtue is never solitary; it always has neighbors." In other words, virtue is not some self-satisfying thing that a person can achieve on his own. An individual will never attain virtue unless he acquires a certain sense of mutual kindness, a gentleness of spirit toward all things of this world.

Hana-nehan: Flower Nirvana

In 2004, at an exhibition called "One Thousand Years of Nature in Japanese Art: From *Sansui* Painting to Landscape Painting" at the Aichi Prefectural Museum of Art, I happened to see a painting popularly known as "Hayaraigō," which means "the swift descent of Amida Buddha."

I loved the associations that the painting evoked.

The work depicts Amida Buddha escorting the dead to the afterworld. But strangely, this Amida figure is surrounded by a mountain covered in cherry blossoms.

Seeing the image, many Japanese people will immediately recall the great *waka* by Saigyō Hōshi,[4] the famed poet and monk of the late Heian period:

Negawaku wa	Let me die in spring
hana no shita nite	under the blossoming trees
haru shinan	let it be around
sono kisaragi no	that full moon
mochizuki no koro	of Kisaragi month

In this poem, Saigyō expresses his desire to die amid cherry blossoms in full bloom, on the night of the full moon around the fifteenth night of the second lunar month (*kisaragi*). The great artist who painted "Hayaraigō" must have known Saigyō's poem, written a century earlier.

The associative link between cherry blossoms and death goes back much further. The link has, in fact, constituted a vital part of Japanese tradition, ever since the dawn of Japanese myth. According to legend, the god of our ancestors married the goddess of the cherry blossoms, and so we humans, unlike the immortal gods, are fated to live brief lifespans and meet early deaths—our hereditary "link" to our cherry-blossom heritage. Moreover, the notion that cherry blos-

4. Saigyo Hōshi (1118–1190)

soms scatter their petals deliberately, precisely at the moment that our love for them has reached its peak, can also be traced back to a certain poem from the eighth century.

The spectacle of cherry blossoms in full bloom covers the underlining reality of death, and that notion has evolved over centuries. It was Saigyō who sealed this idea with a remarkable poetic evocation of that profound connection between cherry blossoms and death. After this poem, Amida greeting the dead while the cherry trees were bursting with color became a set mandala pattern.

When that association was formed, it was only a matter of fate that subsequent generations of Japanese would come to cherish a deep-seated feeling for cherry blossoms. One of our greatest aspirations as humans, after all, is to end our lives beautifully.

The term *hana-nehan*—*hana* 花 (flower) and *nehan* 涅槃 (nirvana), or "flower nirvana"—seems to me, at least, to distill the essence of those aspirations to die under cherry blossoms. For Japanese people, the very scene of cherry blossoms blooming in ecstatic, wild profusion captures the experience of nirvana in a frame of visual wonder.

There are four distinct scenes that come to mind when I let the image of "flower nirvana" (*hana-nehan*) flow through my imagination.

The first is the famous custom of *hanami*, or cherry-blossom viewing. When cherry trees are in full bloom, crowds of people eat and drink and dance under the cherry trees while they admire the blossoms fluttering in the breeze. It's almost a celebration of their fortune at having been born into a state of nirvana: under cherry blossoms, they enjoy themselves, indulging in scenes of sensuous pleasure and merriment.

Another old belief is the one that falling petals can kill people: that they can throw people into a state of crazed derangement, often resulting in death. If that sudden demise took you directly from the worldly "flower nirvana" straight into actual nirvana, what a blessing that would be!

Yet there is also a second type of "flower nirvana," which exists in the everyday realm. The painting "Yuku Haru" (Passing Spring) by famed Nihonga artist Kawai Gyokudō,[5] which appeared in the same 2004 exhibition, depicts an old man twisting a rope while sitting in a tethered boat under cherry blossoms. The two other boats in the painting are cargo boats that are used for threshing or cleaning rice.

Quotidian scenes of people at work that have taken place for centuries—that much is constant. Testifying to that unchanging history, the surface of the painting presents the quiet stillness and peace of mind that routine affords. The same eternal cycle of cherry trees putting forth their blossoms comes around once a year, like clockwork, after which the limbs scatter the pink blossoms to the ground and eventually bud green leaves—and it all occurs and recurs within the settled routine of everyday life.

Isn't this sense of repose none other than the gentle calm of nirvana itself? Those whose lives have come to an abrupt end will joyfully join the realm of the deceased amid this scene of "flower nirvana." And how lucky they are—for they have literally died and gone to heaven!

The third type involves the scenes of "flower nirvana" that exist within the order of the cycle of the seasons. In *shiki byōbu*, or "four-season folding screens," the spring screen always includes depictions of cherry blossoms. Cherry blossoms seem to have been inputted somatically into our bodies and brains as the signature semiotic emblem of spring; we can't help but feel anxious until the cherry blossoms start to bloom.

By the same token, when the cherry blossoms do start to bloom in spring, and when the leaves start to showcase their colors across mountain canvases in autumn, we embrace becoming enfolded into the great cycle of the universe. By participating in this eternal procession, we achieve a profound sense of serenity—a state of nirvana. Each year, the cherry blossom season ushers the Japanese people into a rapturous pleasure not unlike the so-called "religious exultation" (*hōetsu*), which one derives from following Buddhist teachings.

The Japanese people also hold a strong desire to establish a nirvana in the real

---

5. Kawai Gyokudō (1873–1957)

world, as well: a separate space that exists at a specific, concrete spot. Generations ago, people chose the Yoshino region around the city of Nara as their preferred place for experiencing "flower nirvana." They planted thousands of cheery trees there, as though in imitation of the thousand Buddhist wooden stupas called *sotoba* seen in Kyoto. To this day, people flock in droves to Yoshino in hopes of reaching "flower nirvana."

To date, countless literary and artistic works have taken up the theme of cherry blossoms. The fact that the Japanese people have consistently held such a keen interest in those pinkish flowers is a reminder of a power that continues to call us forth: to a world where the flowers embody the seductive space of *hana-nehan*, forever whispering into our ears.

The Words of Shinran

Shinran and the Contemporary World

More than seven and a half centuries have passed since the great Japanese Buddhist monk Shinran[6] died. And yet, not once during that long span has Shinran's name been forgotten. His teachings are more necessary now than ever before, in fact.

Generations of Japanese called Shinran "Shinran-san," out of a special sense of intimate respect. I always attribute his enduring popularity to the fact that virtually everyone has something to say about him. (Forgive me for using the phrase "Shinran popularity," but it is appropriate given the man's tremendous popular appeal and charisma.) This feeling of familiarity has continuously kindled affection for this great religious figure.

I, too, am among those who feel close to Shinran and have something to say about him. I've even included a short essay on Shinran's life and teachings in my compiled writings, and I revisit his works every now and then.

When I glance through the books in my bookshelves, I come across many works related to Shinran. Among them is the work by the novelist and essayist Itsuki Hiroyuki[7] called *Tariki: Embracing Despair, Discovering Peace* (2001).

One could argue that Shinran's revolutionary doctrine known as *akunin shōki* (悪人正機) has been central in sustaining his popular appeal over the centuries. *Akunin shōki* is Shinran's famous notion that the primary object of Amida Buddha's powers of salvation (by which humans achieve rebirth in paradise) is not the virtuous but rather the *akunin*—the "sinners" and "evil ones." As he puts it in his *Tanninshō* (Notes Lamenting the Differences): "If a good man (*zennin*) can be reborn in paradise, a bad one (*akunin*) can be all the more so!" (*Zennin nao mote ōjō o togu, iwan ya akunin o ya*). What a radical statement to make! No doubt, careful consideration went into making such a weighty, controversial pronouncement—one that reveals his unprejudiced eye and boundless capabilities!

---

6. Shinran (1173–1263)   7. Itsuki Hiroyuki (b. 1932)

When I wonder just how many human hearts his words and teachings must have saved over the course of history, I start to feel dizzy. It's staggering to me. Indeed, I'd say the number must be in the hundreds of millions, maybe even billions.

In my view, the various recondite theories about Shinran's life are of little practical value. Few people have willingly relinquished as many personal possessions as Shinran did. He gave away all of his belongings, even the clothes on his back, virtually renouncing even the last remains of food in his stomach. Certainly, the conviction to discard one's every last belonging is a hard conviction to keep. When people would ask him how they should conduct themselves during their short times on this earth, his response was always the same: "Recite the sutra!" By "sutra," of course, he meant the *nenbutsu*: "Namu Amida Butsu," or "I take refuge in Amida Buddha." That's the phrase central to the Pure Land school of Buddhism in Japan. It goes without saying that his teaching transcends time.

Yet it is also equally obvious that both people and the world have lost their original vitality to an unprecedented degree over the last few decades. Such spiritual impoverishment has few equals in history. What we humans must now do is jettison our attachments to superfluous things, search out more authentic modes of experience, and aim to live a fuller, richer life that meets our essential needs rather than simply going on with the conventional way of living.

This does not mean, however, that we should strive to live or act in a forced, unnatural manner. We simply must combine our own natural energies with those of everyone else in order to find a way to go on living together in harmony.

The great calligrapher Hibino Gohō,[8] in his final work, left these words before departing from this world: "There is a supreme joy to be felt when we blossom together in unison." This notion of "blossoming together" in collective unison is precisely the meaning of *tariki*, the method of salvation through the "power of another."

8. Hibino Gohō (1901–1985)

When everyone blossoms together in collective fellowship, it is wise to follow Shinran's lessons. Plainly stated, you should simply relax and release the tension in your shoulder. This method of *tariki*—relying on the "other powers" for salvation—does not mean, of course, that we should simply let ourselves fall into laziness or sloth and wait passively for rapture. On the contrary, "blossoming in unison" requires even more effort than does the path of *jiriki*, or reliance on "one's own strength," which seeks to attain salvation alone.

The *Tannishō* (*Notes Lamenting the Differences*) and the *Kyōgyōshinshō* (*The True Teaching, Practice, and Realization of the Pure Land Way*)

The most important literary work in Shinran's corpus is no doubt his magnum opus *Kyōgyōshinshō* (The True Teaching, Practice, and Realization of the Pure Land Way), which was completed around the year 1224. But I strongly advise that people should also read and savor his extremely concise treatise *Tannishō* (Notes Lamenting the Differences), which comprises a series of interview notes transcribed by the famous monk Yuien[9] just before Yuien's death. This work cemented the legacy of Shinran for later generations.

It's relatively easy to read, too. Having set his heart to the task of educating and enlightening the masses, Shinran came to dislike the fastidious self-reliance doctrine of *jiriki* (自力), which holds that it is possible to attain salvation through "one's own strength."

With that in mind, it's time to examine Shinran's renowned *Kyōgyōshinshō*. The work's title consists of four Chinese characters—*kyō* 教, *gyō* 行, *shin* 信, and *shō* 証—suggesting what are probably the four essential components of all religions: teaching (*kyō* 教), action (*gyō* 行), belief (*shin* 信), and testament (*shō* 証). The thrust of the book, needless to say, is the subject of belief (*shin*).

In particular, Shinran's teachings urge people to rely not on their own strength but rather on the strength of Amida Nyorai, or "Mida" as Shinran sometimes called this celestial Buddha. He went even further, insisting that people's faith in the saving power of Amida should occupy an unconscious realm, so deep down that they aren't even aware of their own dependence. You can see just how important belief was for him.

---

9. Yuien (dates unknown)

For example, here is a passage from the *Kyōgyōshinshō*:

The master spoke: "Trust constitutes the foundation of the way [. . .] Where there is trust, there can be no heart that is defiled with earthly dust [. . .] Trust allows us to bestow charity upon the needy, begrudging nothing. Those with trust joyfully enter into the Buddhist law. Trust fosters and increases wisdom, meritorious deeds, and virtue. Those with trust will always eventually reach the realm of the Nyorai, the realm of enlightened ones. Trust effectively purifies all sensory perception. When the power of trust is fortified and hardened, people will experience none of the three sufferings. Trust thoroughly and everlastingly annihilates worldly desires (*bonnō*) at the root. Faith properly and single-mindedly seeks out the blessing (*kudoku*) of the Buddha."

I wish I had enough page space to elaborate further. For the purposes of my discussion here, though, note that he manages to repeat the word "trust" (*shin*) a total of nine times in this short passage. By "trust," of course, he means trust in the Primal Vow, which is the only means by which one can attain supreme enlightenment.

Why exactly did Shinran preach the importance of faith so powerfully? Another passage from the "On Faith" chapter states the following:

What a pathetic creature I am! I, Gutokuran, taking my name from that foolish bald mythical bird known as the *ran*, drowning in the vast ocean of sexual desire, seduced by the great mountain of fame and repute (*meiri*), finding no joy despite having entered the ranks of enlightened ones, incapable of enjoying my approach to the pure land. How shameful! How piteous!

Obviously, the subjects of this passage—amorous desire (*aiyoku*) and worldly repute (*meiri*)—are natural concerns for all humans. But those corrupted, morally compromised people among us, those who get tangled up in the concerns of the mundane, have no capacity for self-enlightenment. No matter how hard they might try, they cannot avoid getting caught up on the "ordinary path," and so avoiding that ever-tempting road is not something they can do on their own strength alone. Helpless and "devoid of strength," they have only one recourse: to put their faith in the merciful hands of Amida Nyorai.

And yet, some will say, Shinran may have espoused such teachings—but didn't he contradict himself when he decided to marry a woman? Didn't he live a longer life than most people of his era did? Isn't he just a hypocrite? You might raise those criticisms, but Shinran would not have seen your objections as evidence of contradiction.

In fact, Shinran discusses this very issue in the chapter "On Faith." Humans cannot avoid illness and death. Those who are fortunate enough to have a skilled doctor and access to good medicine can have their illnesses treated and be healed. In Shinran's lexicon, these benefits can also be achieved through what he calls *monji* 聞治, which literally means the "sutra-listening cures."

The Buddhist term *monji* means to cure one's afflictions by listening and heeding Buddhist law—that is, to develop a devout heart simply by listening repeatedly to the six-character chant of "Namu Amida Butsu" of Amida Nyorai.

Shinran did not positively affirm lust (*aiyoku*) and worldly fame (*meiri*). He just asserted the vital importance of knowing that faith always proceeds from a state of sadness and hardship, which arise out of our insatiable, spirit-drowning desire for love and fame.

It is only natural that religion should seek to elucidate the nature of belief and faith. But the singular uniqueness of Shinran's thought is that he places his own sadness—the sadness of "Gutoku," of being the "bald fool," as he called himself—at the opposite side of faith.

Shinran in the Minds of the Japanese

To me, this way of thinking about salvation and suffering is even more essential in the disenchanted, spiritually impoverished age in which we now live.

Today, in Japan, the sadness around us represents a crucible for forging a new kind of faith (*shin*)—precisely what Shinran instructed humanity to do.

It once occurred to me that the masses of Japanese people must have breathed a tremendous collective sigh of relief when the Jōdo Shinshū school—True Pure Land Buddhism—first appeared in Japan in the thirteenth century.

After being transported to Japan in the mid-sixth century by Seong of

Baekje,[10] Buddhism had come to be an ideological weapon of the state, used to stabilize the new royal authority and pacify the country. This tradition persisted for several centuries as a kind of fortuitous arrangement between the imperial court and the Buddhist authorities. But for the general masses, that convoluted relationship made the doctrine hard to readily comprehend. Ideological "state Buddhism" lacked the proper utility in providing salvation to the anguished hearts of the people.

At that point, Hōnen[11] and Shinran came down from the mountain to expound a new teaching to the people. I imagine the common folk were over-joyed, grateful to learn the joyous blessings and virtues of the Buddha.

After encountering brutal government suppression, Hōnen and Shinran both eventually had to flee the capital. Shinran went on to tread the arduous, lonely path of the revolutionary pioneer. But the development of culture is a curious thing. It can only take root after passing through multiple configurations and permutations; no cultural phenomenon can last unless it undergoes these nec-essary stages of transformation. After all, culture is something that solidifies its roots through frequent social transitions, which continuously both reinforce and modify it. This is the nature of all forms of culture, religion included.

After his death, Shinran's philosophy continued to spread through succes-sive generations of Japanese people in a continuous, unbroken line. Though the majority of Japanese people today claim to have no religion, they often unwit-tingly find themselves intoning to themselves the *nenbutsu*: "Namu Amida Butsu." "I take refuge in Amida Buddha," they say. In our current times, which are fraught with great peril and drastic upheavals, we should once again embrace the teachings of Shinran and endeavor to seek out new modes of living. And the only way to find those new, restorative modes of living is through the crucible of pain and suffering.

---

10. Seong of Baekje (r. 523–554)   11. Hōnen (1133–1212)

Unbearably Light Ashes: On Gyōki

I once visited a certain temple in Ikoma City in northwestern Nara Prefecture.
The temple is called Chikurinji.

I visited the temple because it's the burial site of the monk Gyōki,[12] one of
the best-known priests from the Nara period (710–794). The stone monument
in front of his grave is large and formidable, but the grave itself is hardly impressive. It just sits there inconspicuously amid a natural stand of trees. Here, Gyōki
came to slumber for all eternity, his eventful life having been brought to a close.
When I let it all sink in, when I know that his spirit resides there before me, an
overwhelming feeling fills my heart.

Gyōki's life ended on the second night of the second month of Tenpyō 21—
the year 747 in the Western calendar. His cremated body was apparently interred
six days later, on the eighth day. His remains were stored in a silver bottle, which
was put in a four-tiered vessel, which was then put in a two-layered bronze cylin-
der, which was then enclosed in a stone coffin. The epitaph on the bronze cylin-
der is said to spell out the circumstances of Gyōki's burial.

According to the epitaph, Gyōki's disciples turned toward the remnant bones
that had just been consigned to the cremation flames and, in chorus, looked sky-
ward and began to wail in lamentation. But by this point, Gyōki's *utsushimi*—
that is, his "mortal, transitory self" or "present existing body"—was no longer
there. Only the ashes of his bones remained. As the inscription on his epitaph
reads:

> No matter how much we press ourselves against the great master's remaining
> bones and weep and mourn, our tears are futile. We strain our eyes but see
> nothing. All that remains are these crumbled brittle bones (*shari*)—and yet
> even these are nothing but unbearably light ashes.

12. Gyōki (668–749)

The last line strikes me as particularly poignant. It says that the remains of his cremated bones were no more than "unbearably light ashes" (*kotogotoku karuki hai nari*). It wasn't simply because Gyōki was eighty-two years old at the time of his death, a frail body of meager weight. Rather, the unbearable lightness of his ashes served as physical proof of his suffering and hardship.

Some say that one can detect visible physical differences in the textures of cremated bones, which supposedly vary depending on how much pain and tribulation the person experienced during his or her lifetime. The bones of a person who lived a life of intense suffering, the theory goes, will immediately turn brittle and crumble apart. The phrase "unbearably light ashes" eloquently captures Gyōki's life, which he lived under inordinately heavy, soul-crushing hardship; the words evoke an almost soul-crushing weight with a graceful, poetic touch.

Gyōki was appointed high priest (*daisōjō*) at the age of seventy-eight in the year Tempyō 17 (745), ostensibly because the ruling regime needed his assistance in erecting the famous Daibutsu (Great Buddha) statue at Tōdaiji in Nara—a project that Emperor Shōmu[13] and the Minister of the Right (*udaijin*) were fervently promoting at the time. What's more, it also seems that Gyōki was not at all pleased about the construction plan. In the epitaph I cited above, you can also find this revealing statement:

> There was a time when Gyōki was assigned the high-ranking position of Chief Monk in the Office of Monastic Affairs (*sōgō*). He served in that particular capacity for some time. But despite this promotion, he showed no interest in such worldly concerns as rank and status.

Instead, Gyōki always stood together in solidarity with the common people. The masses were his natural community, his natural place of action. Like magic,

13. Emperor Shōmu (701–756)

the people would congregate around him, follow his teachings, and thereby help propagate the Buddhist dharma or law. Those who struggled in their everyday lives would make their way through the crowd to congregate around the monk.

This tremendous popularity was unacceptable from the government's standpoint. When Gyōki was fifty years old, the government ridiculed him as a "green, petty acolyte" (*kozō*) and denounced his teachings.

Despite the antagonism, Gyōki's congregation of followers continued to swell. In the second year of the Tenpyō era (730), the sixty-three-year-old Gyōki had apparently managed to expand his group of several thousand followers to as many as ten thousand.

Gyōki, together with his multitude, excavated ponds and ditches for irrigation. They erected bridges and repaired roads. They set up facilities and *fuseya* lodging houses for travelers to lodge in. There were stories that he purchased boats to enable his impoverished followers to cross rivers.

The ordinary people held Gyōki in such high regard that they even dubbed him the "Bodhisattva Gyōki." Wherever he stopped to rest would thereafter become a training base (*dōjō*) for people to practice and teach the faith; the "Forty-nine Monasteries and Nunneries of Gyōki" correspond to that network of training facilities for studying Gyōki's interpretations of Buddhist dharma.

Gyōki was constantly engaged, living among the salt of the earth—the "dust of this world," as the Buddhist expression has it—as a kind of private missionary to the masses. Not once did he ever bend or yield to government repression. His charisma must have been extraordinary. To be sure, there were many Nara-period monks who came to win public admiration, such as the monks Rōben[14] and Dōji.[15] But Gyōki was in a league of his own. He possessed a completely different make-up that made him the undisputed leader of the people.

There is another passage from his epitaph that reads: "I now near the end of this life of chosen suffering, having reached the age of eighty-two."

This sentence sums it all up. Mindful of Gyōki's life and teachings, his humble commitment to suffering, I always find myself reflecting on the profoundly moving, inspiring phrase "unbearably light ashes" whenever I recall Chikurinji in Nara.

---

14. Rōben (689–773) 15. Dōji (?–744)

APPENDIX

NOTES

1 Adapted from Donald L. Philippi's translation in his *Kojiki* (Tokyo: University of Tokyo Press, 1968). The original text appears in Nishimiya Kazutami, ed., *Kojiki, SNKS 27* (Tokyo: Shinchosha, 1979), p. 169

2 Matsuo Bashō (1644–1694), Japan's most famous poet.

3 Adapted from Steven D. Carter's translation in his *Traditional Japanese Poetry: An Anthology* (Stanford, CA: Stanford University Press, 1991).

4 Adapted from Edwin A. Cranston's translation in his *A Waka Anthology, Volume One: The Gem-Glistening Cup* (Stanford, CA: Stanford University Press, 1993).

5 Adapted from Helen Craig McCullough's translation in her *Brocade by Night: "Kokin wakashu" and the Court Style in Japanese Classical Poetry* (Stanford, California: Stanford University Press, 1985).

6 Adapted from Steven D. Carter's translation in his *Traditional Japanese Poetry: An Anthology* (Stanford, CA: Stanford University Press, 1991).

7 *The Ten Thousand Leaves: A Translation of the Man'yōshū, Japan's Premier Anthology of Classical Poetry*. Volume One, trans. by Ian Hideo Levy (Princeton, N.J.: Princeton University Press, 1981).

8 Adapted from Anthony H. Chambers's translation in Haruo Shirane's *Traditional Japanese Literature: An Anthology, Beginnings to 1600* (Columbia University Press, 2007).

Nakanishi Susumu was born in Tokyo in 1929. After graduating from the University of Tokyo, he remained at the university to pursue graduate studies, earning his doctorate in literature in 1959. In 2013, he was awarded the Order of Culture, Japan's top prize for cultural contribution. His pioneering work on the *Man'yōshū* (*The Ten Thousand Leaves*, completed in 759 CE)—Japan's oldest poetry anthology—from an East Asian perspective garnered critical attention, eventually leading to his being awarded the Yomiuri Prize for Literature in 1964, the Japan Academy Prize in 1970, and the Watsuji Tetsurō Culture Prize in 1991. His study of *Genji Monogatari* (*The Tale of Genji*, early eleventh century), which employed the same critical framework, prompted a change in readers' values and won him the Osaragi Jirō Prize in 1998. His book *Nakanishi Susumu no Man'yō Mirai Juku* (Crash Course on the *Man'yōshū* for Children, 2005) won the Kikuchi Kan Prize in 2010. At the same time, he continued to explore the nature of the Japanese ethos, publishing a quick succession of books on the key themes of love, death, madness, and wandering. Starting in 2001, he published his three-part series *Nihonjin no Wasuremono, Ichi kara San* (Things Japanese Forgot, in Three Parts), which neatly summarizes the ideas developed in his previous books. His writings on the *Man'yōshū* are all included in his eight-volume anthology *Nakanishi Susumu Man'yōshū Ronshū* (A Collection of Essays on the *Man'yōshū*, 1995-1996), while his other writings can be found in the six-volume anthology *Nakanishi Susumu Nihonbunka o Yomu* (Nakanishi Susumu's Readings on Japanese Culture, 1995).

In recent years, Professor Nakanishi has devoted his energies to the task of elucidating the *kokoro* ("heart" or "mind") of the Japanese people in three key works, *Kokka o Kizuita Shinayakana Nihonchi* (The Pliant Japanese Intelligence that Built a Nation, 2006), *Nihonjin Ishi no Chikara* (The Will Power of the Japanese, 2009), and *Jō ni Ikiru Nihonjin* (Japanese People: Living by Feelings, 2013), culminating in his general theory of the subject in his *Kokoro no Nihon Bunkashi* (A Cultural History of *Kokoro*, 2011). From 2007 to 2013, Shikisha published the thirty-six-volume anthology *Nakanishi Susumu Chosakushū* (Complete Works of Nakanishi Susumu), which includes virtually all his works published prior to 2006. His previous academic positions include Professor at University of Tsukuba, Professor at the International Research Center for Japanese Studies (Nichibunken), President of Osaka Women's University, and President of Kyoto City University of Arts. He has served three terms as member of the Science Council of Japan and three terms as member of the Japanese Language Council. He has been appointed poetry composer (*meshiudo*) for the annual Utakai Hajime (First Poetry Reading) held on January first at the Tokyo Imperial Palace. In 2004, he was recognized as a Person of Cultural Merit. In 2005, he was awarded the Order of the Sacred Treasure.

Professor Nakanishi has also been very active abroad, serving as visiting professor at various prestigious institutions in China, Princeton University in the United States, and the University of São Paulo in Brazil. He played a pivotal role in reviving Nalanda University in India, subsequently serving on its executive board of directors for nine years.

Ryan Shaldjian Morrison is a literary translator and scholar of Japanese literature. He is currently a tenured lecturer at Nagoya University of Foreign Studies. Born and raised in Phoenix, Arizona, he received his first M.A. in Japanese literature from Arizona State University in 2004, his second M.A. in Japanese literature from Sophia University (Tokyo) in 2009, and his Ph.D. from the University of Tokyo in 2016 for his dissertation on the modernist writer Ishikawa Jun. His nearly completed monograph explores Ishikawa Jun's early works, focusing on their antagonistic relation to the founding principle of modern Japanese literature: *shajitsushugi* (realism). His blog on Japanese literature is called *Behold My Swarthy Face.*

（英文版）『美しい日本語の風景』他所収
The Japanese Linguistic Landscape: Reflections on Quintessential Words

令和元年8月21日　第1刷発行

著　者	中西　進
訳　者	ライアン・シャルジアン・モリソン
写　真	中西　貴美子

発行所　　一般財団法人出版文化産業振興財団

　　　　　〒101-0051　東京都千代田区神田神保町3-12-3

　　　　　電話　03-5211-7282（代）

ホームページ　https://www.jpic.or.jp/

印刷・製本所　　大日本印刷株式会社